RVing to Alaska

Cover design by Nick Inglish

RVing to Alaska
© 2010 RV Stuff

ISBN 978-0-9825682-0-0

First Edition
Printed in the United States of America

For information, contact:
RV Stuff
1116 Sea Pines Drive
Savannah, Texas 76227
940-368-0068
alaska@aboutrving.com

All rights reserved. This book or parts thereof may not be reproduced or used in any form or by any means—graphic, electronic or mechanical, including photocopying, recording, taping or information storage and retrieval systems—without written permission of the publisher. Making copies of this book, or any portion, is a violation of United States copyright laws.

Table of Contents

About this Book vii

About this Author xi

Planning For Alaska 1
   Thinking About Going 1
      Summer 2007 2
         Notes on My Planning 4
   My Plan 4
         Notes on Driving 6
   Time Allocations 7

Our Route 7
    Our Route Maps 9
    Some Thoughts About Our Route 16
        Notes on the Original Route 18
    Not on Our Route 19
        We Didn't Go to Chicken 19
        We Didn't Go to the Arctic Circle 20
    Not The Only Route 21

Where to Find Info 23

    Fulltiming Required 23
        More Info about Allocating Time 24
    Must-Have Books 26
    Websites 28
        Notes on Other Travel Websites 31

First, Some General Info 35

    Mile Markers 36
    Road Conditions 37
        Notes on Preventing Rock Damage.38
    Where to Pull Off 40
    Packing Extra Stuff 41
    Tools, Tires, Filters, Things, Stuff 42
    Some Other Generic Hints 43
        Notes on Evening Entertainment 46
    Emergency Road Service 48

Personal GPS Tracker...49
General Campground Info..51
    Notes on Campgrounds......................54
An Assortment of Travel Tidbits..............................55
    Wildfires...55
    Weather 55
        Notes on Weather Averages...............56
    Visitor Centers 56
    Border Crossings 57
    Confirming Border Crossing Info 57
    Have Pets? 58

Canadian Info...59
    Driving Info...60
        Notes on Ferry Travel.........................60
    A Lesson on Frost Heaves.................................63
    Canadian Campground Info............................66
    Money, Credit Cards, General Info 69

Some Canadian Places to Go....................................73
    ALCAN (now Alaska) Highway 74
    Dawson Creek, BC..76
    After Dawson Creek, BC 77
    Fort Nelson, BC 78
    Liard River Provincial Park.............................79
    Watson Lake, YT...80

Whitehorse, YT 82
The Cassiar Highway 85
    Notes on Driving the Cassiar Highway   86
Route 37A or Turning West to Hyder/Stewart 88
Hyder, Alaska 90

Alaskan Info 95

Highways in Alaska 98
Where to Pull Off 98
Campgrounds in Alaska 100
This is Not a Travelogue 101
    Alaska Samboree 102
    Moose Dropping Festival 103
    Be A Tourist 104

Some Alaskan Places to Go 107

Valdez 108
Whittier 110
The Kenai Peninsula 110
Homer 111
    Pratt Museum 112
Soldotna 113
Seward 114
    Seward Museum 115
    Alaska SeaLife Center 115
    Kenai Fjords National Park 116

- The Iditarod 117
- **North of the Kenai** 118
  - Reindeer Farm..119
  - Musk Ox Farm 119
- **Anchorage**..120
  - *Notes for Military People*..................120
  - Ship Creek State Hatchery 121
  - Alaska Aviation Heritage Museum 121
  - Anchorage Museum..122
  - Anchorage Farmer's Market 122
- **Denali National Park**..122
- **Fairbanks** 124
  - Fairbanks Visitor Center...125
  - University of Alaska Museum of the North.......125
  - Alaskan Pipeline..126
  - Fairbanks Ice Museum..127
  - Summer Solstice Celebration 128
  - Midnight Sun Baseball Game 129
  - Gold Dredge No. 8...129
  - El Dorado Gold Mine 129
  - Riverboat Discovery..129
  - Creamer's Field Migratory Waterfowl Refuge...130
- We Learned Something and Had Fun......................130

Say Bye-Bye 131
- My Focus..132

About this Book

"RVing to Alaska" is the only book focusing on "how" you can make the trip to Alaska by RV with just a smidgen of travel guide tossed in.

It's different than any other trip. Since you will drive your RV to Alaska, there is specific RV-related information relevant to both Canada and Alaska. This is information that, unless you have taken an RV to Alaska previously, will likely be new and different.

Lots of other information and pictures is available in my Alaskan blog. My blog is more of a travelogue about what to see plus a bit of the "how to" information in this book and contains lots of pictures embedded in the flow of text—not just a separate collection or slide show. My blog and this book overlap a bit.

However, my blog is not some daily journal and definitely not a "feel good" piece for my friends. It is often where I "test" the material for books like this one. I recommend you go online and read about our trip at…

rvstufff.blogspot.com

(Note… there are three "f's" in this website.)

The majority of information in ***"RVing to Alaska"*** is about the differences between RVing in the "Lower 48" and **northern** Canada/Alaska. These three distinct geographic areas have different laws, traditions, and each has a measure of uniqueness to it. With that, you will learn about such things as driving over frost heaves, road conditions, routes, emergency road service, where to go, visitor centers, pets, wildfires, border crossings, packing extra stuff, campgrounds, loonies and toonies, boondocking sites, wildlife, credit cards, historic mile markers, and moose droppings to name a tiny few of those differences. Those differences were the basis for this book. I was surprised at some of them but interestingly, never disappointed.

So, this book is about what Sandy and I did to plan for and pull off this major trip. There is no speculation about things we did not experience firsthand. For example, we did not stay in any public campgrounds around Anchorage. I'm retired military so we stayed at the FAMCAMP (military-speak for campground) at Fort Richardson. This military installation borders the city of Anchorage.

As another example, we, unfortunately, did not see any salmon running. While this was one of the main things we both wanted to see and experience, it did not happen while we were there. So I cannot write about it.

We were told the reason was that Alaska had a late snowmelt (due to an extended winter), the rivers/streams were low, and the salmon had not started up the rivers to lay their eggs—therefore., no salmon runs. It was so bad that Alaska Fish and Wildlife temporarily banned salmon fishing—commercial and private—for a period of time while we were in the state.

They did have a salmon run in the Kenai Peninsula about three weeks after we left. That never caught up with us so we never saw those rivers "teeming" with salmon swimming upstream. (This is a reason to go back!)

Therefore, I'm sorry, but I cannot comment on salmon running with two exceptions. You will find these in the *"Alaskan Info"* section late in the book (p. 95).

I am amazed by the number of e-mails I receive from RVers asking questions about going to Alaska. My blog sort of started this explosion of questions. Of course, mentioning the Alaskan trip during our seminar presentations all over the nation would also set off a number of questions.

Finally, being curious, I tried to find any book on traveling to Alaska by RV but there wasn't any. There were a handful of campground-recommendation books and a bunch of travelogue-type books and videos on how great Alaska looks—some good and some a waste of money. But I believe this is the only book devoted to "how" to plan and make the trip to Alaska by RV.

We did it. It worked. It was wonderful. You can, too.

Let me know what you think.

R. E. Jones
alaska@aboutrving.com

About this Author

I've been doing this a long time—camping on wheels—since 1962. Sandy (spouse) and I have been fulltiming for several years. We meander everywhere across the USA and Canada in our diesel pusher. I stay busy. Here's my info...

Ron has retired (several times). He is retired Army (medical, 1970), retired Senior Professor of Engineering Technology at the University of North Texas (1998), and retired publisher (RonJon Publishing, Inc.) in 2006. Ron's hobbies are traveling, cooking, good wine, photography, writing, and eating out, and enjoying a good, local microbrewed beer.

Ron writes (a lot). He is a columnist for Coast to Coast RV magazine, has had feature articles published in Motorhome, Highways, Family Motor Coaching, and Escapees magazines, and is a contributor to the Good Sam Website (Weekly RV Tips). He has written eight books including numerous textbooks for public schools and colleges, how-to books, co-authored the best-seller RV book entitled *"All the Stuff You Need to Know About RVing"* (ISBN 1-56870-514-X), was a collaborator with Sandy on *"Wrinkle-Free RV Laundry"* (ISBN 978-156870-590-3), and recently released *"Fulltiming for New and Used RVers"* (ISBN 978-1-56870-610-8). Of course, this book, *"RVing to Alaska"* is his newest book.

Ron and Sandy present a variety of RV seminars nationwide at rallies, shows, and various gatherings. From Fulltiming to driving topics to Hand Signals to the now famous "Sewage 101," their seminars are filled with great information, use professional-quality media, are laced with humor, and based on the idea that *"You don't know what you don't know."*

Planning For Alaska

Thinking About Going

Going to Alaska by RV was the culmination of a lifelong goal for me—I've wanted to go there in an RV forever. I have no idea "why" Alaska specifically other than I really like to travel to unusual places and love snow-capped mountains.

Even though we started fulltiming back in 2003, I just couldn't seem to "fit in" an Alaskan trip. My writing and seminars became more and more popular and we kept getting busier every summer attending RV events all over the "Lower 48." The trip kept slipping down my priority list so we put it off—the reason doesn't matter.

To add to the complexity of trying to plan this major venture, we tried to get together with friends to make the trip. It is harder to put together a trip with friends but it is a great way to travel. Planning this causes everyone to work with multiple schedules and commitments. There were originally three coaches that planned to go. However, two of them had to make the decision not to do the trip. Sandy and I had the opportunity (finally) and decided to do it alone.

You have to go when you are physically able. You just never know when health issues will stop you. So, it was an easy decision for us and ultimately worked out just great. The trip, I'm sure, would have worked out equally as well with our friends traveling with us.

Summer 2007

Let me take you back for a moment to Summer 2007 and, once again, we were planning to make a lengthy RV trip to Alaska that next year—2008. Having put this off for the previous three years for various reasons, it's time to go.

What's "lengthy?" My trip will consume the summer. I plan to cross the USA/Canada border going north just before Memorial Day and going south, cross it again about Labor Day. Also, by coming back into the USA during September, we will miss the heaviest tourist traffic since schools will be in session.

We have been to Alaska three times on cruise ships. On two of those trips, we stayed an extra week (on our own—no RV), visited Anchorage, and took the train to Denali National Park. My RV trip will not include the cruise ship stops along the Inside Passage including Skagway and Ketchikan but will include time in Denali.

My "plan" was really loose at this point (in 2007) but I was thinking and doing some things to prepare even though the trip was ten months away. I am not a detailed planner.

If there is an event I want to see, then I'll plan our trip to ensure we will be at the event when it happens. For example, one year we went from Michigan, through Canada via Montreal, up the St. Lawrence Seaway, all over the Canadian Maritimes, and returned through New England six weeks later. The only thing actually planned was to be in Halifax to attend the Royal Nova Scotia International Tattoo on July 1st. We got our Halifax campground reservations several months in advance for that event.

I will make reservations if needed. If we plan to go into a busy area, for example, we will reserve a spot. But I don't do this unless I have to.

Notes on My Planning

I actually do more research than planning. So, I search for things to see along the way and make time to do those plus others that we find simply by being there. I rarely reserve a campsite more than a day in advance since I do not want to have to bypass points of interest just because I have a reservation somewhere.

I am a good researcher and good organizer. I have people tell me they know what campground they will be in on a Tuesday, six months from now. I rarely know what campground I will be in tomorrow.

I could, but don't want the structure and especially don't want to feel that I have to follow a schedule. It's one of the things I love about RVing—the flexibility—to be able to say as we pull out of the campground… "Do you want to turn right or left?"

My Plan

Our decision was to drive our 2007 Monaco Dynasty on this trip rather than rent an RV. Our 42-foot motorhome isn't dinky. We fulltime, the coach is our only home, and we didn't want to be away from our home for three months. We also towed our '04 Saturn Vue on this trip.

Many RVers told us their different plans for getting to Alaska including lots of renting of coaches. One fulltimer told us that they and another couple were going to purchase a Class-C. One couple would drive it up, travel for six weeks, and then fly back to the "Lower 48." The second couple would fly up to Alaska, travel the second six weeks, and then either sell the RV up there or drive it back and sell it here. They were doing this to save the miles plus wear and tear on their respective motorhomes. Interesting.

"Buckshot Betty's" is a typical restaurant along the route. It's small, the food is good, reasonably priced, and you will likely have to share a table with a local. Plus, they typically have parking for a big RV or several. We had a very good lunch here. You won't find many places like this away from the cities and towns.

We decided not to go with a caravan for a variety of reasons. We want to spend more time on this total trip than caravans typically allocate, visit some different places, and really do not need their structure for this type of trip.

There is one thing I really want to see and I lucked onto a website that had the information I need. I learned they had built observation platforms in Hyder/Stewart (more on this later) to protect you from the bears (and the bears from you). The grizzlies, brown bears, and bald eagles show up when the salmon make their run. I really wanted to know when to be there and stumbled onto the information that July and August are the perfect months to visit. Hey, that's great! This fits perfectly with my meandering trip returning south.

Notes on Driving

We don't cover many miles in a given day and that's by choice. Normally, our driving day starts about 11:00 AM because that's when most campgrounds say you should be out. That's fine. Our driving day ends typically around 4:00 PM because that's early enough to get the better parking spots at Flying J, Wal-Mart, and other boondock sites. It works for us.

Plus, that typical day is broken up with a stop for lunch (going in someplace or fixing it in the coach) and stopping to trade drivers. We trade about every 60–90 minutes. It works for us.

Our usual driving day is around 200± miles (322+ km). A heavy driving day is 300± miles (483± km) and if possible, we avoid these. We have had some "killer" days at 400± miles (644± km) but those are very rare—almost bordering on an "emergency" somewhere.

Time Allocations

Our basic route planning was based on bugs and weather (seriously). We wanted to spend much of June in the southern parts of Alaska (Kenai Peninsula). My thinking was that, hopefully, the weather would be good—admittedly, it should warm up there first as it is the farthest drivable area to the south.

From our three cruises to Alaska, we knew that July is a peak growing month in the Anchorage/Denali area. The flowers were in bloom, gorgeous, and nearly every town had giant hanging flower baskets on every street corner.

That would allow us to arrive in Fairbanks sometime late July. We would miss the Summer Solstice Celebration (p. 128) but you cannot do it all—at least not in one trip. The days are long, the flowers are blooming with hopefully, the best of weather and the least of bugs. From Fairbanks, we would start south with at least a month left for this final portion of the trip. Hey, sounds good to me!

Our Route

You will find that my route was slightly different from most. For basic planning purposes, I knew we wanted to spend time in the two major (accessible) cities of Anchorage and Fairbanks (you cannot drive to Juneau). We also wanted to travel over much of the Kenai Peninsula, take a side trip (no RV) to Kodiak Island, see the most possible scenery, and not get too far off the main highways. After all, we have a big rig—42-feet with a GVW about 44,000 lbs.—and we are towing a car. We definitely need to stay on the main routes.

As it turned out, our route was fine all the way. There were two problems. One was construction but this was really minor. The other was frost heaves (p. 63). However, I'd follow this route again and recommend it to others. Here is the brief version of the main route we took north after crossing the US/Canadian border…

- Crossed the border into Canada at Sweetgrass, Montana
- Drove up through Banff and Jasper Parks
- From Jasper, east to Hinton, AB then north to Dawson Creek, BC
- To Tok, AK
- South to Valdez
- Ferry to Whittier
- Drive direct to Homer
- Ferry to Kodiak Island and back (without the coach)
- North to Seward, then Anchorage, Talkeetna, Fairbanks
- Southeast to Tok and on to Watson Lake, YT
- South to Hyder/Stewart
- South to Prince George and Vancouver

While this was our route, it is certainly not the only route. A detailed discussion of other options takes place at the end of this section (See *"Not The Only Route,"* p. 21).

Our Route Maps

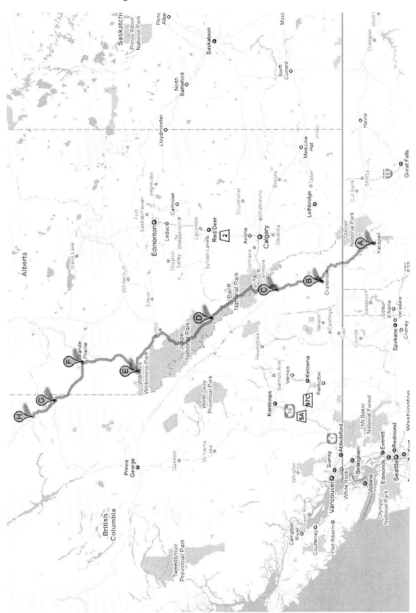

Note that my placemarkers are for mileage plus general route direction and information only. They do not indicate mandatory or planned stops.

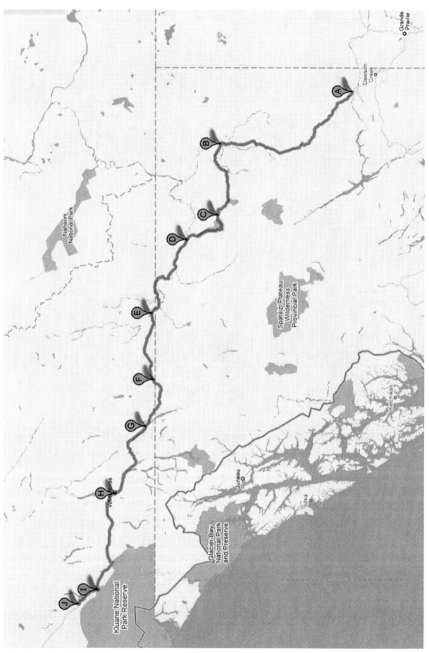

From Fort St. John, BC, we turn more westerly through Canada. This route weaves in and out of the Yukon Territory.

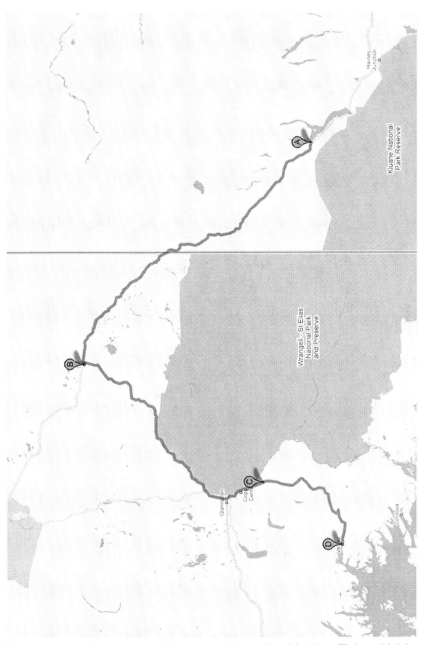

We cross the border into Alaska and head to Valdez. Tok to Valdez is about 250 miles (402 km) but we took two days on this beautiful leg of our journey. Next time I will take three days.

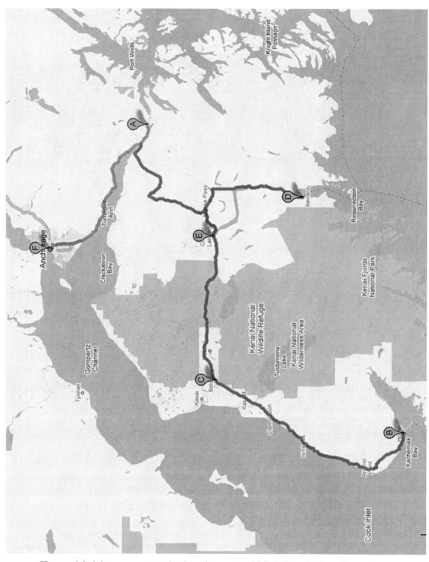

From Valdez, we took the ferry to Whittier (A) rather than backtracking via the highway (more on this later). On the Kenai Peninsula, we did a lot of backtracking but it worked out just fine for what we wanted to see and do. The letters on the map may seem out of order but match our sequence of stops.

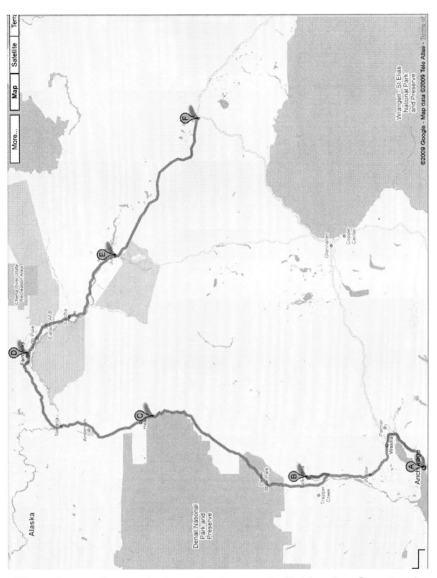

There is no other route from Anchorage to Fairbanks. Our stop in Talkeetna was great (more on this later). From Fairbanks, the logical route to Tok is through Delta Junction. Doing this circle route prevents backtracking.

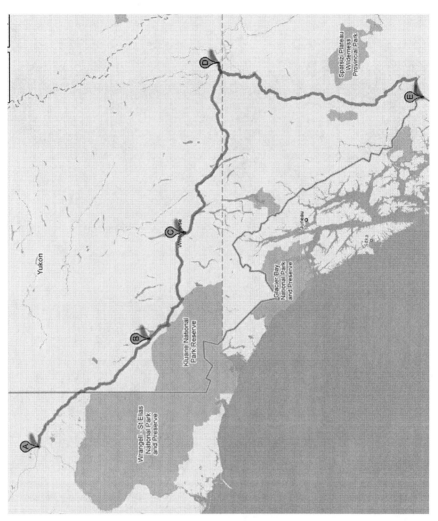

Tok is the Alaskan town you will always visit twice! It's the first town you drive through coming in from Canada and the last town you pass through on your way out of the state.

Going to Hyder/Stewart takes you back into Canada. Our route backtracked about 650 miles (1,046 km) from Tok to Watson Lake, BC but there's no other route to drive there. We just meandered back on this return trip because, by plan, we had not stopped on the way north to do any normal "touristy" things.

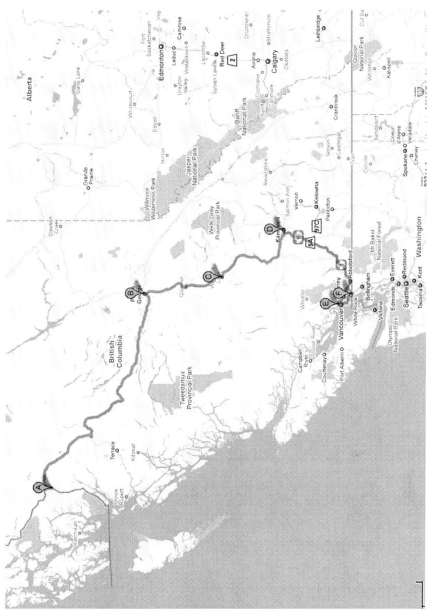

Hyder/Stewart to Blaine, Washington was the last major leg of our trip north of the "Lower 48." There is no shortcut to Vancouver. Be sure to read my warning later about avoiding the shorter route through Whistler, BC. (p. 61)

Some Thoughts About Our Route

We crossed the northbound border in Montana because we had relatives there and had been visiting them. Some RVers speculate on which crossings will be less hassle, less questioning, or maybe just faster and easier. I, personally, think this is nonsense. Every crossing will be easy for some and harder for others. Cross where it is convenient and absolutely don't take any contraband with you.

The basic plan for our Alaskan trip was to not spend much time driving up through British Columbia. We really want to travel more in BC but that will be other trips. About two years ago, we had spent about six weeks going through Banff to Jasper and ending up in Vancouver. Going Banff-to-Jasper again was the best highway north for us based on our Montana crossing location and it didn't hurt that it was a spectacular drive. Our focus will be to spend the maximum time in the farthest area—Alaska.

We headed *east* from Jasper toward Hinton, Alberta and this was a new route for us. The drive from Hinton, AB to Watson Lake, YT (885 miles or 1,425 km) would be new territory but we will stop/stay as long as needed (to be a tourist) in Dawson Creek, Fort Nelson, BC, and Watson Lake, YT. We will not backtrack over this route out of Alaska so this was the time to see what was there—within limits.

From Watson Lake, we will drive on into Tok, Alaska (about 650 miles or 1,046 km) but not stop to be a "tourist" on the way north along this stretch. The reason is that when we return from Alaska, we have to backtrack on the Alaska Highway from Tok back to Watson Lake (there is no other way to drive this).

During that return drive southbound, we will spend whatever time we want visiting this area and there are lots of things to see. Our different return-route will take us south just a bit west of Watson Lake. We will then be on the Cassiar Highway (CA 37—a new route for us). This will result in a quicker trip north and a slower trip south. Not stopping to visit along this 650-mile (1,046-km) stretch on the way northbound will also leave us maximum time in the northernmost areas.

The drive from the Alaska Highway south, on the Cassiar Highway, was different. Much of the time we were driving on this fine two-lane highway that was built up—sometimes 30–40 feet higher than the surrounding landscape. Oh well, the view was good. Other than a bit of construction, this was a good drive.

About 365 miles (587 km) south of the Alaska Highway, CA 37A turns off the Cassiar Highway and goes west to the coast. This is the only driving route to Hyder, AK and Stewart, BC—two small towns situated just across the border from each other. I wanted to visit there.

Hyder may be the only US border town without a customs check. You can't get in or out of Hyder by car without going through Stewart—they do have a Canadian customs checkpoint. Think of it this way... you can drive into Hyder without being checked but cannot drive out.

Hyder is our last chance to see the bears catching the salmon. The grizzlies, brown bears, and bald eagles show up when the salmon make their run. However, our luck with the salmon has not gotten any better but we go to Hyder anyway. It was a good decision.

Notes on the Original Route

My original route was to leave Stewart/Hyder and go to Prince Rupert, BC (on the coast). From there, our plan was to put the coach on a ferry and go over to the northern part of Vancouver Island, then meander down the island to Victoria (this would have been in September), and return to the USA through Port Angeles, Washington. For whatever good reason (I can't remember now), we decided not to do that with plans to make this portion of the trip at another time.

We headed west to Prince George, BC instead and then, CA 1 south through Cache Creek, and finally into Vancouver. We spent a total of 84 days in Canada and Alaska. This was perfect timing and allowed us to see what we wanted, stay any one place as long as we wanted, take our time, and not move occasionally for the mandatory R&R day. Simply, it worked.

Not on Our Route

In conversations and seminars, I am always asked about driving one special side trip. That portion of the Klondike Loop from Chicken, Alaska to Dawson City, BC is known as the "Top-of-the-World Highway."

We Didn't Go to Chicken

My *MILEPOST* says that you can drive from Tetlin Junction (just east of Tok, AK) to Chicken, AK and this 64 miles (103 km) is paved. From Chicken to Dawson City is unpaved (but—*I'm told*—fairly well maintained) and this leg is 103 miles (166 km). Then, Dawson City to the Junction of PH1 and PH2 (just west of Whitehorse, YT) is paved for 323 miles (520 km).

This is a 490-mile (789-km) loop trip we decided to skip since the unpaved portion would be rough on our coach. However, I was also told there are a lot of interesting attractions along that route—very rich in gold rush history.

My decision not to go was based on talking with several RVers about their recent drive on this highway and what to see. The majority concluded that it was like basic training in the military… It was a unique experience but they wouldn't want to do it again!

Specifically, I talked with RVers during our trip to get the most current information on construction or other problems on that specific highway. Nearly all told stories of lots of mud and not much to see when they got there. They told of great scenery but overall, the vast majority were negative about that side trip, i.e., "wouldn't do it again." So, we decided to not drive that route.

We Didn't Go to the Arctic Circle

Heading north, 11 miles (18 km) out of Fairbanks you can connect with the Elliott Highway (Rt. 2) or the Steese Highway (Rt. 6).

If your goal is Deadhorse—a few miles from Prudhoe Bay, your first 70± miles (113± km) on the Elliott is paved. At Livengood, you get on the Dalton Highway (Rt. 11). This (nearly all) unpaved road goes north for 430± miles (692± km) to Deadhorse. It's drivable. We didn't drive it. It is known for the tundra, wildlife, and big trucks and is commonly called "The Haul Road" by locals.

The Arctic Circle is approximately 185 miles (298 km) north of Fairbanks (a 370-mile, 595-km, roundtrip) so you can say you've been there. We chose not to go.

Sorry, you can't drive to the Arctic Ocean. Private vehicles will have to stop in Deadhorse. They are not allowed on the oil fields.

Don't go to the town of Circle. Circle (also called Circle City, pop. 100) is 162 miles (260 km) northeast of Fairbanks at the end of the Steese Highway (Rt. 6). Circle was named by miners in the late 1800s who believed that the town was on the Arctic Circle. The Arctic Circle is actually about 50 miles (80 km) north of the town of Circle.

Before you attempt this trip, be sure to thoroughly read your ***MILEPOST*** about the trip and potential hazards. Also, check with local tours (especially out of Fairbanks) as many of them have bus, van, or flight tours to the Arctic Circle. This would allow you to go there and save the potential damage by not driving your RV.

Not The Only Route

Now, our route is certainly not the only route. We crossed into Canada from Montana only because we have relatives that live in Bigfork—just west of Glacier National Park on the north end of Flathead Lake—about 40 miles (64 km) south of the border. It was convenient to visit our relatives prior to starting our drive north of the border.

As I stated earlier, we had visited the Banff/Jasper Parks area a couple of years earlier so on this trip, we could drive right on through this wonderful area with only limited stops. Plus, the highway was great, too.

Your route and where you complete your border crossing will be determined somewhat by your starting location in the USA. For example, if you were starting from New England, you may want to consider a Canadian route that heads west but is north of the Great Lakes, rather than dip down around Chicago.

Driving this route, you could save a few bucks on a tankful of fuel if you decided to come back into the USA at Sault Ste. Marie, Michigan and cross back into Canada at International Falls, Minnesota but you would only save about 40 miles (64 km). Add two extra border crossings with that route and the potential hassle may not be worth it.

During our years of traveling, we have entered into Canada and returned at a variety of crossings literally from Lubec, Maine (the easternmost crossing point) to Blaine, Washington (the westernmost crossing point). Some are busier, some are tiny, all will question you to some extent. Some have searched our coach to some degree (never emptying it out) and others have looked at our Passport and waved us on. You cannot guess at what will happen to you.

Author Note: It must be strongly noted here that both our international neighbors north and south — Canada and Mexico — have **NO TOLERANCE** for weapons crossing their borders. Don't do it!

There are numerous "weapons" including stun guns, Tasers, batons, and various pepper, bear sprays (some), and other types of sprays. Many/most of these are illegal to take into Canada and Mexico. I strongly recommend that if you decide to cross their respective borders, do your research to find out what you can do legally. You may have your RV searched trying to enter the country. Don't carry any contraband or weapons, period.

I have been told by a retired police officer that a can of wasp spray will act as a serious deterrent similar to pepper spray. His statement was that while he had no proof of the effects on humans, he had witnessed firsthand an incident where it had been sprayed to disentangle two very aggressive fighting dogs.

Where to Find Info

Fulltiming Required

You must be prepared for at least some fulltime RVing (an Alaskan trip is the epitome of extended travel) due to the overall amount of time required for this trip. Seriously, taking an RV to Alaska is not a quick venture. So, if you are going to make the Alaskan trip, you must become a fulltime RVer for a while (see p. 27 for more Fulltiming information). Even if you decide to travel with a caravan, they also require/consume enough time on the Alaskan trip that it becomes extensive—not bad, but just a lengthy trip.

More Info about Allocating Time

I recommend at least two full months at minimum for your trip and three months is even better. Our trip was a bit over 13,000 miles (20,921 km). If we divide that by 60 days (two months), that's an average drive of 216-miles-per-day (348 km)! Yes, it's a long trip but you don't want a fast trip.

Whitehorse, Yukon Territory, has one unique weathervane—a retired, full-sized Douglas DC-3 aircraft and it turns with the wind!

Using a full ninety days is even better. Our trip lasted 84 days north of the USA/Canadian border and we were completely satisfied. One accepted rule of thumb is that you should be *south of Whitehorse* (Yukon Territory, Canada) on both Memorial Day and Labor Day. Doing this will (hopefully and historically) prevent you from being in one of the early (or late) freak snow storms. Whitehorse is pretty far north and winter comes early and lasts a long time.

One professional RV caravan company's shortest Alaskan trip was 32 days but *that trip started* from Dawson Creek, British Columbia (BC). Just to get to Dawson Creek, BC from various places in the "Lower 48" adds to the challenge, many miles, and, of course, the time. A quick bit of research showed the following mileage from a few major cities across the USA. Consider this…

- Seattle to Dawson Creek, BC is 800+ miles (1,287 km)
- Denver to Dawson Creek, BC is 1,600+ miles (2,575 km)
- Dallas to Dawson Creek, BC is 2,500+ miles (4,023 km)
- Atlanta to Dawson Creek, BC is 2,750+ miles (4,426 km)
- Boston to Dawson Creek, BC is 3,000+ miles (4,828 km)
- Orlando to Dawson Creek, BC is 3,200+ miles (5,150 km)

Keep in mind **this is only one-way mileage** and must be added to their actual "caravan" miles! Again, the total mileage is significant—but worthwhile!

Those professional caravan companies typically end their tours at some Canadian city—it may be different from where you started. From there, you may go directly back to your home (or home base). That will add even more time to the total trip.

For example, if we use Dallas as the home base (starting and ending point) for the 32-day venture, doing so would add 5,000 miles (8,046 km) to this 32-day caravan (Dallas to Dawson Creek to Dallas)! Therefore, you need at least a couple of months to do a minimal Alaskan trip. After all, it's a long way, will take lots of time, you will have to spend extra funds to complete this, so you want to do it right!

My purpose here is definitely not to discourage anyone but to help you accurately plan, prepare, and complete this major trip. It is a wonderful, delightful, spectacular, and inspirational RV trip. I absolutely recommend it but don't do a quickie!

Must-Have Books

The first three books are **absolutely necessary** for this trip. The remaining recommendations are very helpful and worthwhile. Consider the following and as they say, *"Don't leave home without it!"*…

- *RVing to Alaska* (this book)… is the newest and (we believe) only book combining some travelogue with lots of pure "how to" information. From carrying spare parts to cracked windshields to permafrost, learn the tricks of Alaskan travel by RV.
  rvstuff.org or aboutrving.com

- *The MILEPOST*… Legendary Alaska trip planner and travel guide to the highways, roads, ferries, lodgings, recreation, sightseeing attractions, and services along the Alaska Highway traveling to and within Alaska, including Alberta, British Columbia, Northwest Territories, and the Yukon. Don't try to get by cheap here and use your friend's copy from last year. The businesses up there change all the time and you want the latest, correct information. You can plan with an older version but get the most up-to-date edition. Get it late March when the new edition is printed.
  milepost.com

- *Traveler's Guide to Alaskan Camping*… Mike and Terri Church have personally visited over 400 campgrounds throughout Alaska, the Yukon Territory, and Northern British Columbia. You get complete coverage of the routes north, including the Alaska Highway, Cassiar Highway, Alaska Marine Highway, and the Klondike Loop. They include full campground descriptions, maps showing exact locations, and all contact information.

     rollinghomes.com

- *Bell's Travel Guides*… Their *Mapbooks* provide a massive amount of practical northern travel information. These comprehensive books are useful guides available for people traveling to Alaska. There are 65 full color maps of the cities, towns, and highways in the North. Bell's *Mapbooks* are free. You pay the postage. Bell's Guides may also be available in Information Centers.

     bellsalaska.com

- *Fulltiming for New and Used RVers*… by Ronald E. Jones. (One of my books.) Learn how to stay in touch, handle finances, protect yourselves and deal with weapons and valuables, mail, emergency road service, emergencies, personal locators, and just stuff you need to survive (in style) in your RV for a couple of months on that extended trip or longer. Remember, Alaska is a long trip and you will be fulltiming for a while.

     rvstuff.org or aboutrving.com

- *Alaska*... by James Michener. I read this novel back in 1989 before my first cruise to Alaska and it provided a wonderful, interesting, and accurate background (and a great story, too). So, I read it again before this trip. I recommend you do, too. Now, you can buy it used.

- *Public Land's Campgrounds in Central Alaska*...

    This is a *map* and it's only fifty-cents!

    It is difficult to find information about the 100+ public campgrounds on central Alaska's highway system since they are managed by multiple agencies. This comprehensive map eliminates this challenge. An easy-to-read chart details their amenities—from boat ramps and fishing opportunities to the availability of water and dump stations. The map covers the Glenn, Seward, Sterling, Parks, Richardson, Denali, and Alaska Highways.

    Author Note: We did not know about or use this map for our trip but it was strongly recommended by other RVers. You can't go wrong for 50¢!

    alaskageographic.org

Websites

Websites are a wonderful source of information but I always recommend when using private websites, that you try to locate a secondary source to help verify the first one. The content is updated (as it should) and hopefully, you are getting the most current information. That's good.

I've tried to take you directly to the pages within a given site that will provide specific help rather than to a generic address and then forcing you to dig out the information. Website addresses (URLs) change, too. So, if one of these fails to work when you try it, here's a suggestion... Start with the full URL but delete a portion of the web address. Remember, don't erase the .com, .gov, or any other extension. As an example, on the first website try deleting the *"traveler.shtml"* and see if the remainder (**dot.alaska.gov/**) will access the website.

I used the following ones extensively but by the time you go, there may be others as good or better. Just keep looking.

- **dot.alaska.gov/traveler.shtml**... This is the Alaskan Department of Transportation official site and contains tons of information about highways, access, problems, construction, and just about anything else you will need when driving in Alaska. Plus, there is currently a link on this site to obtain a free Alaska Highway Map. Hey, another good map can't hurt!

- **travelalaska.com/index.aspx**... This is currently the state's "official" travel site. Sponsored by the Alaska Travel Industry Association, this site has "everything" Alaskan on it and is a worthwhile planning tool. The organization of this site saves you lots of time.

    Get on their mail list now and (if they are still doing it) they will send you their latest booklet entitled, *"Alaska Official State Vacation Planner."* It's an excellent resource and it's free!

- **hellobc.com/en-CA/default.htm**... You'll be going through British Columbia, so bookmark this one. Sponsored by "Tourism British Columbia"—the provincial Destination Marketing Organization for British Columbia."

- **travelyukon.com**... You will also be driving through the Yukon Territories, so bookmark this one. Sponsored by the "Department of Tourism & Culture," Government of Yukon.

- **www1.travelalberta.com/en-us**... If you happen to pass through parts of Alberta, try this one. Sponsored by the "Government of Alberta," it will provide lots of travel information for Alberta only.

There are a gazillion websites you can use and my plan here is not to dump a large number of them on you. The following are a few I used at various times. As I recall, most were helpful. Remember, websites change.

Notes on Other Travel Websites

In the past couple of years, I have read and gathered lots of Alaskan trip information from two RV-related e-mail groups. I'm active on these groups and people send me all kinds of great information (some of it is very personal—for example, like daily expenditures). I save, review, and appreciate it. I don't have some magic all-encompassing site for this trip so I cannot recommend one. I have found numerous Internet sites that are great. Try all of these long before you head north...

www.akferry.org
Alaska Marine Ferry

www.dnr.state.ak.us/parks
Alaska Parks

www.driveyukon.com/interface.html
Drive the Yukon

www.northtoalaska.com/index.aspx
North To Alaska

www.dawsoncity.ca
Dawson City, Yukon

travelyukon.com
Yukon Campgrounds

www.elp.gov.bc.ca/bcparks
British Columbia Parks

www.britishcolumbia.com/regions/towns/
index.asp?TownID=3952&webregionID=2
Stewart-Cassiar Highway 37 BC

www.britishcolumbia.com/regions/towns/?
townID=3664
Stewart BC

www.google.com
Google

And don't forget my blog…
rvstufff.blogspot.com
(Note… there are three "f's" in this website.)

Of course, websites are changing all the time, new ones are being added, and (if we are lucky) an old one is occasionally deleted. I really don't like to include websites in my writing because of the many ongoing changes. Sites come and go and even pages within sites are constantly being changed. At least we hope so. That access to change means that any serious site will be continuously updated (hopefully) and have the latest information. If you find that any of these sites have changed, consider that an advantage because you will likely be getting newer, more current, information.

There is also an enormous amount of information available from various e-mail groups and individual blogs. These on-line groups have some common interest and you can even find some devoted specifically to Alaskan travel.

Even sites devoted to other topics will have an occasional discussion about Alaskan travel. The downside to the typical e-mail group is that anyone can post anything (within the group's rules) and it is not uncommon that opinions, rather than facts, are the source of information. It's sort of a "buyer beware" mentality so don't believe everything you read on these groups. You may be getting a biased opinion of one person. Be sure to check any information with other sources. It can't hurt. I call it the "President Reagan Method"... *"Trust, but verify."* The same advice is true for individual blogs. Some are excellent, some are nearly useless.

This topic—traveling to Alaska by RV—is of interest to lots of RVers including those going and those just dreaming about it. Quite often, this topic will surface more frequently about March when, it would seem, that RVers are getting anxious to go somewhere.

⟶

Author Note: As shown on the facing page, nearly every RVer will stop at Watson Lake, BC on their way up or back from Alaska. Home of the *"Sign Post Forest,"* this small town has become world famous. Started by a U.S. Army soldier while working on the construction of the ALCAN Highway in 1942, travelers are still adding signs to the collection. It's fun and interesting to read the signs.

If you plan to add a sign, be sure to have it made up before you leave home and bring it with you. Don't forget a hammer/nails or drill/screws to attach the sign to the pole.

First, Some General Info

There are many similarities in traveling through Canada and the USA. But, when traveling through both countries—as you will have to do—it's good to know the unique differences about both places. I have traveled in Canada many times and have a great deal of respect for Canadians and their wonderful country.

The information in this section seems to be more applicable the farther north you are traveling. Think of it this way... The following information starts after you enter Canada. The farther north you go—especially north of Jasper and the park—the more critical this information becomes. This is due to the fact that you will be entering into vast areas where there is little population, fewer vehicles, tiny towns, and lots of wildlife (who assume they own the highway). Or, it's just very different up there than it is down here in the "Lower 48"—nothing bad here, but just different.

Mile Markers

You will find mile markers along the total route. The exception is where they have been temporarily removed for construction projects. We found that secondary roads even had markers. However, you should note that we were on very few secondary roads in our RV.

The mile markers in *The MILEPOST* are an excellent method of locating about anything along the highways. Some mile markers may actually be addresses. The mile markers have been around forever, are ingrained in the history of the highways, and are still around today. So, a business may have an address such as… "1020 Alaska Highway." That's likely an original mile-marker number.

From the time it was built, road work would take place to repair **and** straighten out the highway. In fact, nearly 150 miles (241 km) has been eliminated from the Alaska Highway (old ALCAN Highway) so the current highway is considerably shorter today. So, while the historic mile markers may still be used (for addresses), the actual mileage on the historic marker may be way off the mark. For someone to have the historic mile marker address is like a badge of honor—never to be taken away or messed with.

There are newer mile markers, Historic mile markers, and kilometer markers now. When Canada converted to the metric system in the late 1970s, that portion of the highways running through Canada received new markers—kilometer markers!

The good news is that all the old markers were not removed. And more good news is that *The MILEPOST* lists them all. It may seem confusing at first but it will be helpful—trust me on this. You will have to study the instructions in *The MILEPOST* to become comfortable with their system but this effort will definitely be worthwhile and the benefits will be worth the time and effort.

To wrap up all this confusion, you will find that some places (in Canada) will actually have (A) a historical mile marker address, (B) a different old mile-marker number for their accurate location on the highway, and (C) a kilometer-marker number for the correct Canadian location along the highway. Whew!

Road Conditions

If you are driving a motorhome and towing a vehicle, you will need protection for the tow vehicle. Otherwise, the rocks and small stones kicked up by the motorhome will beat it to death—lots of paint chipped and windshields broken. Trust me! I learned this from experience.

Notes on Preventing Rock Damage

In gravel construction areas, simply slowing down is considered the best defense against rock damage. When you drive at a particular speed, rocks can be thrown up by your rear tires. These can cause damage underneath your RV (especially a motorhome). They can also cause damage to your tow car.

The large construction trucks typically do not slow down and when they pass you (going either direction), they may kick up larger (golf-ball size or larger) rocks. The best defense here is pulling to the far right when being passed by oncoming vehicles, and, always, slowing down.

However, having said that, *you must be extremely careful on the gravel (construction) sections of highway not to pull too far to the right.* You must not run off the gravel edge. This gravel edge is somewhat loose and may cause you to drop off the road. There is no shoulder.

Some motorhomes may need special protection underneath. Depending on the particular engine/radiator configuration (especially in some diesel pushers), rocks can easily damage your radiator. There are rock guards available to help protect the underneath.

Both in Canada and Alaska, the summer highway "construction/repair" season is short, intense, serious, and busy. Note that all the major highways we were on were paved—yes, regardless of rumors, it's paved. I believe that the rumors about "unpaved" highways are started because of the lengthy construction projects. We saw one sign that said... *"Extreme Dust, Gravel Areas for Next 60 km"* (about 37 miles). This was a lengthy highway-repair project where they were removing the paved surface and repaving the highway among other things. Yes, it had been paved but now needed extensive repairs (plus widening or whatever). So we found ourselves driving on gravel. The gravel was smooth but dusty. You will have to slow down. It will help.

Slow down! If the person behind you is in that big of a hurry, maybe they should have left yesterday!

Author Note: We did not have any damage to our motorhome as a result of gravel, rocks, or anything else. None. I couldn't find a single rock chip.

I had made the decision to not add any protection other than my solid rock guard across the rear and under my motorhome. This decision was a result of talking with many motorhomers that had made this trip. About half said they added additional rock guards/shields/screens (some purchased, some homemade) and about half said they didn't do anything. Some had damage, some did not.

We did have a bad experience with our car. I had lots of chipped paint along the front and leading edge of my hood, my windshield had six big "stars" where rocks had hit. I had the equivalent of a small bucket of rocks scattered around and laying on every nook and cranny of the engine area. We tried to blow these off with an air gun but ended up just picking them off by hand. Luckily, there was no engine damage as a result of rocks being lodged. However, when I go up there again, I will add some type of shield to better protect the front of the car. A piece of carpet will protect the windshield.

Where to Pull Off

Let me define *"Rest Area."* The official Rest Area usually has trash containers, rest rooms (maybe), and often some information (sign or plaque) about that location, geographical area, or historical note. They may also include a building with a visitor center. Generally, they are large enough to hold numerous vehicles of any size.

Let me define *"Pull-Off."* A pull-off is a designated place to pull off the highway. Some will hold dozens of vehicles and some are tiny and only hold one small car. Often you can't see the size of the pull-off without actually driving in.

Many of these sites are "double-ended," that is, have an entrance and exit at each end. This is an important piece of information for the motorhome driver or if you are towing a large RV. With the double-ended sites, you can get out without having to turn around. Trust *The MILEPOST* on this information. You cannot see the exit without pulling in (or driving by) the pull-off.

Packing Extra Stuff

We overpacked with "Just in Case!" basic stuff for Alaska. This included a spare Sani-Con (sewage macerator) discharge hose plus three, 25-foot, ¾-inch garden hoses. I

could dump my tanks nearly 125 feet away. We had a 50-foot, 30-amp extension cord, a heavy-duty 25-foot, 15-amp extension cord (10-gauge, 3-wire), and 150 feet of lightweight extension cords (we use these for our seminars). So, I could plug in about 100 feet away and temporarily, about 250 feet away. Plus, we had three spare 25-foot (white) water hoses so we could get potable water 100 feet away.

We never needed nor used any of the spare stuff—not one piece, not a single time. That's a good thing.

I also thought I would take a spare coach tire with me but could not locate one in time. I called the major tire dealers in Anchorage and Fairbanks to see if they had my size in stock—just in case. They did not. They said it would take about two weeks to get one shipped in. Oh, well, we never needed a spare tire either.

When we make the trip again, I would not take a spare tire—I can wait two weeks. I would take the spare parts simply because I continue to carry them now (remember, we fulltime). I believe the decision was prudent, the extra parts were not expensive, and took up very little space. Going into unknown areas while better prepared is a logical/smarter way to travel—especially with the distances involved here.

Tools, Tires, Filters, Things, Stuff

I took my normal array of tools with me to Alaska, but remember, we fulltime. Therefore, these same tools go with me everywhere. The only thing "special" I purchased to take with me (because we were going to be some distance away from normal service) was an extra length of air hose. I had a

30-foot length and bought another one. This extra hose allowed me to reach all the tires on my tow car without unhooking it (my air chuck connection then was at the front of my motorhome).

I do recommend extra filters and belts for the engine, generator, and AquaHot as these can be changed by roadside assistance. Those with diesel pushers often carry a spare set of filters and belts for their engines and generator. Even in the "Lower 48," a service facility may not have the exact part you need in stock. Carrying a spare set solves this problem.

I had a full engine and generator service (oil/lube/filters) done at the start of our trip. Based on the number of miles or hours since your last engine/generator service, you may need this done while up north. Carrying a correct set of filters would be prudent since having a set (or even a single filter) sent in would be time-consuming and expensive.

I also purchased several bottles of windshield-washer concentrate to take. We are still working our way through it!

Some Other Generic Hints

What follows is a number of unrelated tips that will help you on this trip. Some of these do not apply to other "normal" trips and these also range across borders. They are not specific to Canadian nor US travel. They should help.

Specifically, these tips are "more" applicable when you are north of Jasper Park…

- You see very few cars on the highway the farther north you go.

- Fire up your generator and run all of your roof ACs while driving over any dusty roads. Doing so will establish a positive air pressure inside the coach and help keep the dust out. Don't forget to check your AC and generator filters later. They will likely need cleaning after miles of dust.

- With 21-22 hours of sunlight, trying to make the room dark is difficult so sleeping can be a problem. We bought some inexpensive dark-blue polar fleece cloth, cut it to size, and used the larger plastic clamps to attach it to the windows when we went to bed. It worked really well.

  If you don't want to sleep in the total darkness, clamp the cloth up a bit and leave a crack at the bottom of the window for light to come through. Don't forget to cover the skylights, too. Use the polar fleece cut to size and attach with Velcro.

- You **NEVER** set a bag of trash, or cooler, or food container outside or put one in your car (visible in the window) because you will be visited by a bear who **WILL** get to that bag. Yes, bears are everywhere and yes, bears know what those containers look like. Even if your cooler looks different,—suppose your friends bought you a cooler that looks like a motorhome—the bears can still smell the food.

- There are lots of dump stations located at groceries, towns, gas stations, museums, all over—usually free. Often, there is (identified) potable water close by. So, you can camp cheap by boondocking and there are a gazillion places to do that.

- Wildlife is everywhere. I topped a hill at about 50 mph (80 kph) and three bison bulls—full grown and at least 1,000 pounds each—were grazing ten feet from the pavement. In the Yukon, they call these "speed bumps."

- You will see lots of black bears especially in northern Canada and Alaska. We probably averaged seeing one per day. They were playing along the highway.

- Moose will just saunter out onto the pavement whether a car is coming or not. Moose apparently do not "react" to vehicles like other animals. They seem to just ignore any vehicle regardless of its size or speed. Don't tangle with a moose—you will lose.

- Throughout much of Canada and Alaska, your cell phone will not work. If you are outside a service area, there is no "fix" for this. Check with your provider.

- Check with your cell phone service provider to find what it will cost to make or receive calls while you are in a service area within Canada. Some providers will have some pretty steep charges for these international calls. You don't want any surprises.

- If you have a DVR (digital video recorder—the devices for recording TV shows), then record a large number of shows to take with you. We took about 35 hours of recorded shows and movies.

Notes on Evening Entertainment

You will likely "run out" of TV reception, that is, your US-based service (DIRECTV or DISH Network or something else) will work for some distance north of the US/Canadian border—but not very far.

Although DIRECTV is unobtainable in Alaska, I was told that DISH Network is possible as far north as Denali Park, if you carry a 30" or larger dish. Note that the satellites are very low on the horizon so some parts of Anchorage have reception blacked out by nearby mountains. Even with a working satellite, you will commonly find yourself in tall trees—again, virtually impossible to receive a signal from anything. You may also need to request a change in satellite to ensure a connection.

You may also get a small handful of channels using your roof-top antenna when you are near the bigger cities. However, don't have high expectations that this will work as you will likely be disappointed in the one or two "snowy" channels. Check to see if you can have your DIRECTV or DISH Network service stopped temporarily and save a few bucks since you can't use it anyway.

If you are a reader, I recommend taking lots of books. Sandy and I read every day. So we scrounged through many used bookstores for months before the trip started and literally packed and took a boxful of books.

I also saved up 2–3–4 months of several magazines I regularly read and took these.

I cannot speak to radio reception as we never have it turned on. I was told that Sirius satellite radio works in Alaska except where mountains get between you and the satellites

We borrowed about 30 movies from family members and took these with us.

Emergency Road Service

One common type of special RV insurance is called "Emergency Road Service." It is designed to provide financial assistance, technicians, or professional help for minor emergencies while you are on a trip. I highly recommend this, have carried it on every RV, and have used it when needed. It is inexpensive—often less than $100.00 per year. My emergency road service provides coverage in Canada but not Mexico. Before you purchase, ask if you are covered in these two countries. If you are never going to travel outside the USA, it's not an issue.

Emergency Road Service provides you with help for those common mishaps such as running out of fuel, towing, or flat-tire service. On a large motorhome, it would be extremely rare for anyone to have the tools on board to enable them to change a tire. It is also rare that you would even carry a spare. Therefore, the service is invaluable—especially for the cost. But, as always, read what you are paying for before you buy. Consider these commonly included services…

- **Flat-Tire Service**… Qualified technicians are dispatched to change a tire and may include locating and delivering a new tire.

- **Towing to the nearest Service Professional**… May pay 100% of RV towing fees to the nearest independent professional service center. Actual towing distance may be unlimited.

- **Emergency Fuel Delivery**… Typically, five gallons of fuel will be delivered.

- **Lost Key & Lock Out Service**… A pre-paid locksmith is dispatched to your location.

- **24/7 Toll-Free Emergency Dispatch**… You can always reach a real person.

- **Roadside Repairs**… A mobile mechanic is dispatched to make minor roadside repairs to your vehicle.

- **Trip Interruption Help**… Reimbursement for meals, rental car, and lodging if your vehicle is disabled due to a collision. Typically, you must be over 100 miles (161 km) from home.

- **Protection For Household Vehicles**… May include cars, pick-ups, SUVs, motorcycles, and even boat trailers.

- **Spouse & Children Protection**… May include spouse and children under 25 years old living at home or attending college.

- **Emergency Medical Referral Service**… Assistance with personal or medical emergencies related to an accident or illness while traveling.

Personal GPS Tracker

Even while meandering around the "Lower 48," I have always been concerned that I might break down somewhere without cell service and no satellite (online access). In preparation for our trip to Alaska, my concern increased. Completing that trip proved there were many lonely miles where something could have happened. I was on one stretch of highway in northern Canada that had a sign warning drivers that it was 166 km (103 miles) to the next services. Nothing happened and that's good.

In researching an alternative method of contact for emergencies, I found a product called the SPOT—a personal GPS tracker. The product is primarily sold and marketed to back-country hikers/backpackers. It's small (7 ounces), the size of a fat cell phone, and you use it when you need it.

There are three message options on the SPOT. You set these up on a password-protected web page. The first two are your custom messages and I put mine below to show how the buttons are to be used. The message from the "911" button is automatic.

- **Check In**... *"I'm just checking in—everything is OK! Ron"* (I send this from wherever we parked for the night. Still do.)

- **Ask for Help**... *"Need HELP - likely broke down. Not bleeding so NO 911. No cell. No e-mail. Send help to coordinates. Ron/Sandy."*

- **Alert 911**... When you hit the "911" button, SPOT acquires its exact coordinates from the GPS network and sends that location plus a distress message to a GEOS International Emergency Response Center every five minutes until cancelled.

Whenever the "Check In" button is pushed, a brief e-mail goes to all recipients you have entered into the system. The recipient can click on the link in the e-mail and our exact location shows up on a Google map. I'm glad we had it and glad we didn't use emergency services.

General Campground Info

- Some campgrounds may be full but there's always another choice usually not far away. Caravan companies will reserve numerous campsites in a campground. If so, that campground may fill. That same caravan may be leaving soon (tomorrow?) so ask when you call the campground.

- Every gas station, restaurant, and bump in the road seems to have an "RV park." (I use the term loosely because some looked pretty crude. We would not stay at some of them.) You can easily find campgrounds without making advance reservations. Doing this also allows you to be far more flexible in your travel schedule. There were a couple of times when the park we called to stay in was full but that was rare. Plus, boondocking sites are plentiful.

- Many campgrounds will have a do-it-yourself RV wash on site. This "wash site" may simply be a water hose—typically in the far corner of the campground. Take advantage of these to at least remove the layer of mud and dirt from your RV and toad. Also, we occasionally found campgrounds that allowed RV washing right in your campsite.

- Make sure you reserve a campground for any major holiday week-end. It seems most of Anchorage is somewhere on the Kenai for July 4th and Labor Day. Canada also celebrates Labor Day (they invented it) the first Monday in September (like us) and other Canadian holidays, too. Their campgrounds will fill so to ensure space, you must reserve in advance!

- 50-amp apparently does not exist in many (most?) campgrounds up there. Be prepared for 30 amp, sometimes just 20 amp, or boondock sites (no utilities), and some campgrounds may not have any sewer hookups available at all. We saw places advertised as campgrounds with no utilities whatsoever—not even a single dump site! The reality was that this so-called "campground" was just a grassy area where you could park for a fee. No, we didn't use any of these.

- Living with 30-amp is easier up north because you will rarely need to run the air conditioners plus the sun is shining 21–22 hours per day. Just watch out when running two or more high-amperage-draw appliances simultaneously, e.g., air conditioner, microwave, convection oven, hair dryer, coffee pot, etc., as the 30-amp circuit is easy to trip.

- Although somewhat expensive, you might consider carrying an Autoformer (voltage booster) to help stabilize and boost the power in many campgrounds. Many RVers carry a portable 30-amp model.

- Many older campgrounds are small, very tight, and heavily treed. Be prepared to drive carefully. I have seen our driver's side neighbor so close that their picnic table was sitting over our sewer connection. There were numerous occasions where we could not put out the awning. Your neighbor was that close to you. However, this was unusual.

- There are several city-run campgrounds. We found one in Homer, Alaska plus one of the more well-known ones is in Seward. As shown here, you just find a place, park, then put your fee in the "Iron

Ranger." This is no-frills boondocking (no hookups) but typically comes with a great view—at least it did in Homer and Seward. I believe the cost was $15.00 per night when we went.

- Elks and Moose Lodges are an option for members.

Notes on Campgrounds

While much of this information seems negative, don't use that as an excuse for not making the trip. Many great campgrounds are available with large sites, full hookups, and easy access. Plus, we found that the nightly rates were quite reasonable. We were not in one location long enough to consider discounted weekly or monthly rates. If you are, you should certainly ask.

What we did not find was the typical resort-type campground with the variety of amenities. Apparently there's just too much to do in Alaska so the assumption is that you don't need to be "entertained" by a variety of scheduled activities. Even the one campground operated by Princess Cruises was basic.

Read more about this one in my blog…
rvstufff.blogspot.com
(Note… there are three "f's" in this website.)

An Assortment of Travel Tidbits

Wildfires

Alaska has wildfires as do all forested areas. With the vastness of the state and the fact that only a small portion is accessible by highway, it is unlikely you will actually see any fires or even be close to them when driving. You may, however, find yourself in the smoke resulting from wildfires.

If you have a health condition that is affected adversely by smoke, as an RVer, you can just leave. That may be the most prudent thing to do. That is, simply drive away—to where the air is clear. This may not have been in your plans but it is certainly one solution. Local weather stations may provide radar coverage of smoke-covered areas.

Weather

We visited Alaska during one of the rainiest summers ever—but we had virtually no rain. I recall only two days of rain during our total trip. This was luck. However, we spoke with numerous RVers that spent many days in the rain. We learned that the average temperature for Anchorage in July and August was 64/65° F (18° C).

Notes on Weather Averages

To find weather averages for nearly any major city, worldwide, do a Google search for "average temperature, *city name, state/country*" (put in the correct city, state, or country). Put in the commas, Leave off the quotation marks. You can search Google for nearly anything using this process.

Visitor Centers

I strongly recommend you stop and take advantage of the Visitor Centers—the government/municipal-run ones. They will have excellent and current information that can be invaluable to you whether going on down the highway or staying in an area for a while.

Talk to the people working in visitor centers. They usually have massive amounts of information about the local area and can make your stay significantly better and easier. They know the local information and you don't. Their advice is worthwhile and useful.

Additionally, they will have a wide selection of brochures, maps, and information—sometimes too much to digest.

Border Crossings

Remember, you must enter into Canada to drive to Alaska. There are a few things you should do to prepare for crossing into Canada. All are simple and all are important.

- Get the Canadian insurance form issued by your insurer. One for **each** drivable vehicle (RV and tow vehicle).

- Take your Passport. Make sure it won't expire before you cross back over the border on your way back to the "Lower 48." This is especially important if you are planning on staying up there for two-three months. You have to cross back into Canada to return to the "Lower 48."

Confirming Border Crossing Info

Three websites will provide lots of up-to-date information about the crossing requirements into Canada and back into the USA. They will contain information about border crossings, traveling with animals, contraband, prohibited items, documents, and other information you may need for your particular needs. These are…

- U.S. Customs Agency
  cbp.gov/xp/cgov/travel

- Canadian Border Services Agency
  cbsa-asfc.gc.ca/menu-eng.html

- Go Northwest (a private, non-government site)
  gonorthwest.com/Default.htm

Have Pets?

- Vets are few and far between. If your pet has medical problems, take that into account.

- Put emergency contact information and a picture of your animal somewhere in the coach—sort of a "mini passport" for your animal. If the animal has an identification chip, include that information.

- Have proof of current vaccination for pets.

- If you have an animal more exotic than a dog or cat—look into special entry requirements for both Canada and the USA. Some are subject to quarantine when **reentering the USA**.

- If you feed them special food, bring enough to feed the animal for the entire trip because you might not be able to get it in Canada or Alaska.

Canadian Info

I know you were planning an "Alaskan" trip but there are helpful things you need to know about the lengthy drive north and south through Canada. If you drive the round trip to Alaska and back, at minimum, you will have to drive through portions of British Columbia and the Yukon Territory. Depending on where you cross the border, you may also have to drive through some parts of Alberta. If you are going to drive to Alaska, you will definitely drive though a significant portion of Canada.

We often talk with people during our seminars who tell us they have no plans to go to Canada. Then, we ask for a show of hands for those planning to go to Alaska and many of those same people put their hand up. Think about it… to get to Alaska, you drive up through western Canada and then (well, sort of) turn left.

Driving Info

The shortest driving route through Canada to Tok, Alaska from the "Lower 48" is from Sumas, Washington (a border crossing located a bit northeast of Seattle). Google shows the distance from Sumas to Tok to be 1,834 miles (2,952 km)—one way. Therefore, you must plan on spending several nights, eating several meals, and fueling up a few times in Canada—whether you want to or not!

The alternative is to put your RV on a ferry. You do not cross the international border (entering into Canada) on the ferry—an expensive option—but a great trip.

Notes on Ferry Travel

If you put your RV on a ferry, you must turn off the propane. So, make sure you know the length of time your fridge will stay cold without power.

You cannot stay in your RV while it is on the ferry. Pets cannot leave the car deck and without special permission, you will not have access to the car deck while the ferry is underway.

dot.state.ak.us/amhs/pets.shtml

However, the following information will focus on the driving trip from the USA/Canadian border to Alaska. Consider the following information about driving in Canada...

- If you are close to Vancouver, BC, north or southbound, **DO NOT** consider driving Canada RT 99 that passes through Whistler even though it is a shorter route. It is a narrow two-lane with one-lane bridges and some 16–18% grades.

- Canada is metric. Many RVs have a button that converts their odometer to kilometers and back to miles as needed. We found this to be handy, saved us lots of mental converting, and made it easy for us to be under the speed limit.

- In Canada, *"The MILEPOST"* will list all highway locations/distances in kilometers (km). You will need to pay attention to this when calculating driving times and distances.

- If you happen to use Google maps to plan some of your driving distances, you can easily change between miles and kilometers. When you are on the "Get Directions" page, click on the "Show Options" link. You will have a choice and must select Miles or Kilometers.

- The Canadian highways leading to Alaska are nearly all two-lane highways and they are, for the most part, good roads. We have been up and down lots of 8% grades, some 10%, and a couple of 12% grades.

- How tall is your RV and what does it weigh? All the clearances (weight and height) in Canada are given in metric (kilograms and meters).

So, you never measured it and you really don't know the correct height of your RV. Okay then, let's suppose you are driving down the highway (in Canada) and you see these clearances (above). What do you do? Stop, get out the calculator, and convert these clearances from English to metric to see if you fit? Oh, and did you remember that the conversion formula was 1 foot = 0.3048 meters?

- Measure the exact height and weight of your RV, convert that to meters and kilograms, and put a small sticker on your dash with both the English and metric height and weight (some RVers have a small plastic sign made). Otherwise, you won't remember your metric height/weight next summer. Since this is a critical measure (plus an expensive and potentially embarrassing mistake), you do not want to just guess!

- We covered one stretch of 104 miles (167 km) with no services—no buildings of any kind that we could see—just wilderness. The lesson here is... Keep your fuel tank at least half full. However, there are lots of fuel stops available. Certainly don't run it way down.

- The last 125 miles (201 km) of Canada—from Burwash Landing, YT to the Alaskan border—is famous for frost heaves. These are humps and  depressions in the pavement as a result of the permafrost melting/shifting (see next photo). These frost heaves create a driving hazard that will launch a motorhome into the air or break an axle on a towed RV. (There's more on this below.)

A Lesson on Frost Heaves

It's hard to wrap your mind around the fact that you are driving over permanently frozen ground (permafrost) because the landscape looks normal with trees, plants, rocks, lakes, streams, etc. But that upper layer (I don't know how deep it is) is providing insulation for the permafrost (the permanently frozen ground underneath).

If you scrape away the top layer, this allows the permafrost to melt and it turns to mush. The highways are literally built on top of the layer and the freezing/thawing of the permafrost underneath creates the frost heaves in the road surface. They've tried to solve the problem since 1942 when the military built the original ALCAN highway. It's still not solved.

One 125-mile (201 km) stretch of highway in the Yukon had the poorest roads of the entire trip from Texas. We were warned that the melting and refreezing would make the highway full of ruts (parallel to the highway) and frost heaves (sunken areas and small humps perpendicular to the highway). There were immediately plenty of both. It was a real test of the shocks, air bags, and driving skills!

The ruts were 2–3 inches deep and 6–36 inches wide running a few feet to maybe 50–100 feet along the road surface. (From 5–8 cm deep and 15–91 cm wide and 15–30 meters long.) If you missed seeing them (thus allowing you to steer around it) these ruts would pull your tires/vehicle into the "groove" and you just had to fight it until the rut ended.

You couldn't take your eyes off the road. If you missed slowing down for a frost heave, it would nearly launch the front wheels of the coach off the ground—even driving about 35–45 mph (56–72 kph). There were small orange flags marking many frost heaves but hundreds had no warning.

Occasionally, you would see one orange flag on one side of the road. While I could not verify this, it appeared that the frost heave would be more prominent on that side of the road (with the flag). Steering to the other side seemed to help. With virtually no traffic from either direction on this highway, crossing lanes was a reasonably safe maneuver.

As shown in the following photo, you might be able to spot a frost heave because the painted center line or edge line appears to weave slightly from side to side. The flags were easier to see but there were a number of frost heaves that were not flagged. There were literally thousands of frost heaves in that 125 miles (201 km).

Hitting these at some given speed will cause "porpoising" where the vehicle is sort of floundering up and down. This is when your luck is bad enough that you happen to be going the "correct" speed, there are at least three frost heaves, they are spaced to match your wheelbase length, and you didn't see them. If/when this happens, each "dip" will be coordinated to launch the coach higher and higher. One analogy is that your coach will act like a person on a trampoline—bouncing higher and higher. Don't do this.

Don't take this or any frost heave information lightly. However, if you do, you will change your mind after driving over the first one.

Canadian Campground Info

Here are a variety of suggestions when traveling through northern Canada. My experience is that most of this information does not apply within about the first 200+ miles (322+ km) north of the US border. It seems as though the "rules" are different the further north you go in Canada—nothing bad, but just a bit different.

- A campground (yes, a real campground) may not even have a **central** dump station. However, you will find lots of dumping places at fuel stops, towns (municipal sites), museums, etc. This is very different from the "Lower 48" but a nice-to-know option.

- It is common for businesses (restaurants IF you eat and fuel stops IF you fill up) to offer a boondock site for a night—just ask—it typically won't be posted. We stayed free at a restaurant parking lot in Burwash Landing, YT (dinner was good). We were told we could spend the night at the General Store in Teslin, YT. There were many options and places to boondock.

- We spent the night at Mukluk Annies and **hopefully you can, too** (about 8 miles or 13 km north of Teslin, YT). It cost us $18.00 CD for fresh grilled salmon (or a steak), salad bar, baked potato, beans, bread, a brownie AND free boondocking next to the lake AND a free do-it-yourself RV wash AND a free boat ride on the lake. What a deal! The salmon was fine. There were about 30 rigs there boondocking that night. It is a well-known spot for overnighting. The sad news is that they were closed during 2009. Check it out.

- Most TV satellites will stop working about 100+ miles (161+ km) north of the border between Canada and the "Lower 48." If yours works farther north than that, feel lucky.

- Most of the time, your TV antenna is useless.

- Campgrounds typically had narrow lanes to drive to your campsite. Many of these campgrounds have been in place for several years and it's almost impossible to drive through without trees brushing the side of your RV. Watch for this even though you can't totally avoid it.

- We found several "campgrounds" that were just a plain, bare gravel lot or patch of grass. Yes, they charged you to park there. We did not stay in any of these but they do exist. There were others (like Jade City) that invited you to stay overnight for free on their "patch of grass." Interesting.

- Our experience was that campgrounds had gravel entrances, sites, and lanes and therefore, were dusty (assuming no rain) or muddy (assuming rain).

- Unverified… Through several phone calls and websites, I tried to find the "official" word on parking overnight in pull-offs and rest areas in both British Columbia and the Yukon—but no luck. There are different answers from everyone—even from different offices of the RCMP.

  In some pull-offs, they put up signs stating *"No camping or parking overnight."* The most common situation was the vast majority of parking places did not have any signs. I also searched online and even looked at map legends for guidance. But no luck.

  One government brochure said that it was illegal unless otherwise posted. We interpreted this as it was only okay to spend the night if the sign stated that it was okay but we never saw a single sign like this. We boondocked in several locations and did not have any problems. Our assumption (again, totally unverified) was that if there was no sign prohibiting it, that it was okay. We saw others staying overnight, too.

  Don't assume our experience is blatant permission for you to stay in these. You really need to check on this, too. I'd appreciate it if you would let me know if you find anything concrete on this question.

- 30-amp is far more common than 50-amp in northern Canadian campgrounds. Occasionally, just 20-amp is available. I will pay for 30-amp but not for 20-amp. To me, it just isn't worth it. I can live far more comfortably (without being as careful and monitoring which appliances are in use) by boondocking and using our generator.

- The Canadian federal government agency responsible for administering the national parks in Canada is called "Parks Canada." The Canadian parks and system are similar to our national parks and system in that they have set aside numerous unique protected areas for future generations to visit.

  Parks Canada will require you to purchase a park pass. You can choose a day pass or annual pass. Make your decision based on your itinerary. Also consider the National Historic site pass.

  Provincial parks in Canada are beautiful and all over the place. They are definitely worth a visit. Some have hook ups, many do not. Typically, they are very clean.

  You **may** be able to camp in the park using an RV but you must research this first—before you show up at the gate. The following website will take you to a page where you have a choice of searching the parks by province or by attribute. The "attribute" option will allow you to see what amenities are available in what park plus the maximum size of the allowable RV before you reserve a space.

  pccamping.ca/parkscanada/en

Money, Credit Cards, General Info

- We made it through Canada (both up and back) and did not exchange any money. Everything possible was charged to a credit card. We had only one instance where we were required to use cash (US currency). We purchased two cans of vegetables in a local, small grocery and they did not take credit cards. They took the US currency and gave us a fair exchange rate. The total purchase was only about $2.00.

- If you are not going to exchange any money, take an excess of small US bills. Lots of $1's, $5's, $10's, and $20's are best for payment in small businesses if you insist on using American money. Also, if you insist on using American money in another country, don't complain about the exchange rate. It's their country.

- Many Canadian businesses will accept US bills but not coins. In northern Canada, change will most likely be made in Canadian money. Although our focus in this book is northern Canada, an interesting note is that many Canadian businesses close to the US/Canadian border will have a checkout register that has two cash drawers—one for Canadian money and the other for US money.

- Canadians commonly use two coins, called the "loonie." and "toonie." The $1.00 coin has a picture of a loon on it and became known as the "loonie." When the $2.00 coin came out, it was nicknamed the "toonie"—short for "two loonies."(Keep the "T's" together—toonie = TWO—and you will keep them straight.) The loonie is brass colored. The toonie has a silver outer ring and a penny-sized brass section in the center.

- If you use a laundromat in Canada, it will typically take loonies.

- Your credit or debit cards will typically work at ATMs in Canada. Check with the company that issued your cards to verify if there are any fees associated with using the ATM. Sometimes there are.

- Find a credit card that *does not charge* an "International Processing Fee" or other fee with some such name. Most cards do! Typically, it is about 3% of your total charges. I have a Capital One credit card I use for international travel only. It does not charge any fees for international transactions. However, I make it a point to re-verify that fact every time before we travel internationally.

- Generally, Canada has higher prices than the "Lower 48" for food (both groceries and eating out) and always for fuel.

- Fuel is purchased by the liter (litre) in Canada. For your sanity, think of a liter as really close to a quart. The quick way to think about this is there are about four liters to a gallon. That will get you by and you will be really close. The actual conversion is… 4 liters = 1.056 US gallons.

   So when you see the Canadian station advertising (posting) a fuel price of say, $.90, that is the price per liter. Multiply that posted price times four and you have a pretty close equivalent of the US price per gallon. It's okay to use your calculator if you want to be exact.

- One rule of thumb is that Canadian fuel prices will be about $1.00 higher **per gallon** than US prices.

- You can often call toll-free numbers (800) in the USA from Canadian pay phones without depositing any money. Whatever works!

- Don't assume you can call any USA toll-free (800) number. The phone number can be blocked by the US-based owner of the respective number so that no international calls can get through.

  Do you know if your vehicle insurance claims number accepts toll-free calls from Canada?

- When you get to Whitehorse, YT, stop in at the local city building. They were giving away a three-day parking pass (for cars) so you could park free at any meter or city-owned parking facility. A very nice gesture. I recommend asking your campground if this program is still active and it was active during 2009.

Some Canadian Places to Go

The drive from the town of Jasper (in the Provincial Park) to Watson Lake, YT is 927 miles (1,490 km). This drive was unique to us in that we would **not** return over this particular segment of the route. We had to see and visit what we wanted on the way up to Alaska.

During the first 325 miles (520 km), from Jasper to Dawson Creek, BC, there just isn't much in the way of "tourist" stops or sights to see. So, we rarely stopped along this stretch of highway to be a tourist. The good news was that the highway was just fine all the way. It was an easy drive through rolling country and we saw less and less traffic. This was a new route for us.

ALCAN (now Alaska) Highway

The ALCAN Highway was built during World War II and connects the USA (the "Lower 48") to Alaska through Canada. It stretches from Dawson Creek, BC to Delta Junction, AK (southeast of Fairbanks). Back then, it was 1,390 miles (2,237 km) long but is shorter today due to rebuilding and straightening. The historic end of the highway is near Mile 1422, where it meets the Richardson Highway in Delta Junction, AK, about 99 miles (160 km) southeast of Fairbanks. The ALCAN Highway was later renamed the Alaska Highway.

Construction officially started March 8, 1942 after hundreds of pieces of construction equipment were moved near Mile 0 at Dawson Creek, BC. Construction accelerated through the spring as the winter weather faded away and crews were able to work from both the northern and southern ends. Construction also accelerated after reports of the Japanese invasion of Kiska Island and Attu Island in the

Aleutians. On September 24, 1942 crews from both directions met at Mile 588. That site was named Contact Creek and is located at the British Columbia/Yukon border at the 60th Parallel. The entire route was completed October 28, 1942 with the northern linkup at Mile 1202.

Portions of the highway became a "corduroy road" or log road in the low or swampy areas. This type of road is created by positioning logs side-by-side and perpendicular to the direction of the road. Then, the logs are covered by sand or gravel. The result is an improvement over impassable mud or dirt roads but is a bumpy ride under the best of conditions.

Early on, some 70 miles (113 km) of the ALCAN highway between Burwash Landing, YT and Koidern, YT, became virtually impassable during May and June 1943. The permafrost melted since it was unprotected by a layer of vegetation as a result of construction. A corduroy road was built to restore the route. Corduroy still underlays old sections of highway in the area.

Modern construction methods do not allow the permafrost to melt by building up gravel as a kind of insulation. However, the Burwash, YT-to-Tok, AK section is still a problem. The new highway built there in the late 1990s continues to experience frost heaves (see p. 63).

> **Author Note**: The remaining portion of this section will focus on some things to do and see while driving through the northern portion of British Columbia and the southern parts of the Yukon. I have purposely left out the "lower" portions of Canada—the first 500± miles

(800± km) north of the US/Canada border—because this area is easy to access from the USA. Many RVers visit this area regularly with no plans for going to Alaska. Look on your map or do a search for Prince George, BC. The following will focus on the general area north of Prince George.

Dawson Creek, BC

This is a very nice community and is the home of The Northern Alberta Railway Park (N.A.R. Park). This is the true start —i.e., "Mile 0" —of the original ALCAN (now Alaska) Highway. Within the N.A.R. Park you will find the Dawson Creek Station Museum, the Dawson Creek Art Gallery, and the Dawson Creek Visitor Centre.

There is ample parking for any size RV in the N.A.R. Park. Our coach is shown here (look under the arrow) and the Art Gallery is just across this lot to the right.

- **Art Gallery...** located in a renovated grain elevator and relocated to Northern Alberta Railway Park.

- **Dawson Creek Station Museum...** the west side of the museum building was historically restored to its former life as a railway station, complete with waiting room, office, baggage room, and living quarters.

The Railway Building contains the geological and archaeological history of the areas and a wildlife exhibit with dioramas including a huge mastodon tusk found in the banks of a nearby river.

- **Alaska Highway House...** the story of the Alaska Highway. Located by the Mile '0' Post (downtown).

After Dawson Creek, BC

The drive from Dawson Creek, BC to Watson Lake, YT is 602 miles (964 km). The Kiskatinaw River flows along the east side of Dawson Creek and bends north.

- **Kiskatinaw River Bridge...** Exit east at *MILEPOST* 17.2 (27.8 km) to access the loop road on the Old Alaska Highway. You can drive across the wooden, curved Kiskatinaw River Bridge. It was completed in nine months during 1942–43. The Canadian Corp were contracted to build the bridge, camped in the area, and this became the Kiskatinaw Provincial Park.

At the Kiskatinaw River, a hairpin turn forced the construction of this very unique bridge. Engineers developed this 534 foot-long (162.5 meters) wooden bridge that is sloped and has a 9 degree curve to conform with the bend in the highway.

We drove our motorhome across the Kiskatinaw River Bridge. The weight limit is 25 tonnes (55,115 lbs). Our coach weight is just over 40,000 pounds (18,143 kg). If you are under the weight limit, it is a treat to drive the bridge and about 20-minute detour.

Fort Nelson, BC

The drive from Fort Nelson to Watson Lake, YT is approximately 320 miles (514 km). The highway rises steadily from the vast land of muskeg (like a swamp) and boreal forest to Steamboat Mountain, where the highway leads right into the Northern Rocky Mountains.

- **Fort Nelson Heritage Museum…** Pioneer artifacts, life-size animal displays and a display on the Alaska Highway construction can be viewed, located across the Alaska Highway from the Recreation Centre.

- **BC's most northern traffic light…** located at a pedestrian crossing on the Alaska Highway, be sure to stop.

Liard River Provincial Park

One of the unique and most popular stops on the Alaska Highway is the well known Liard River Hot Springs. These Springs are located in the "Liard River Hot Springs Provincial Park" north of Muncho Lake.

The second largest hot spring in Canada, there are two hot springs at Liard, with water temperatures ranging from 42°–52° C (107°–126° F). The nearest is the Alpha pool and half a mile beyond is Beta pool. Beta pool is larger, deeper, and is likely to have few other people there. It is an easy walk to both pools and they have changing rooms. Bring your own towel.

Watson Lake, YT

- **Signpost Forest...** started in 1942 by a homesick U.S. Army G.I. working on the Alaska Highway, he put up a sign with the name of his home town and the  distance. Others followed and the tradition continues to this day. Today there are estimates between 45,000 and 60,000 signs of various types depicting locations across the world. (See larger picture p. 35.)

  If you plan to put up a sign, have it made before you leave home as there are no facilities here.

  The Signpost Forest is an open area in town, along the highway. It is not manned and is open to anyone 24/7.

- **Northern Lights Centre...** a state-of-the-art video showcasing Yukon's Northern Lights is shown in the NLC's domed 100-seat theatre daily throughout the summer season. Interactive displays explain the science and folklore of the Northern Lights with the latest information about the Canadian space program. Canadian rocket technology played an important part in early Northern Lights research.

Author Note: Even though it is about 90 miles (145 km) from the border, Tok is the first city/town in Alaska after you cross the US/Canadian border going north and the last one you visit on your way back south. There is no other driving route. Everybody driving to Alaska will visit Tok twice!

Also, Tok is where we started to backtrack over the same route that we drove north (on the Alaska Highway)—and you will, too. Just like us, you will have to backtrack about 650 miles (1,046 km) at minimum, and that will take you from Tok, AK almost to Watson Lake, YT. As mentioned previously (p. 16), we did not stop and stay to be a "tourist" going northbound on this part of the route.

During our return drive southbound, we planned to spend whatever time we wanted visiting along this 650-mile (1,046 km) stretch and there are lots of things to see. Doing this resulted in a quicker trip north and a slower trip south through Canada. Not stopping to visit and sightsee along this 650-mile (1,046 km) stretch on the way northbound also left us maximum time in the northernmost areas. For example, we boondocked one night in Whitehorse, YT on the northbound portion of our trip but stayed here six days on the way back.

On the southbound trip, about 12 miles (19 km) west of Watson Lake, YT, we turned off the Alaskan Highway to head south on the Cassiar Highway (CA 37). The Cassiar was a new route for us. (see maps, p. 14 & 15)

Whitehorse, YT

Southbound, the first Canadian city you will visit on the Alaskan Highway is Whitehorse. It is officially located in what is called the "Yukon Territory." (If you do any searching on the Internet, use "YT" for Yukon Territory.) The reason I call Whitehorse a "city" is because it has a Wal-Mart. We could park overnight at this Wal-Mart **with permission**. Be sure to ask. Also note that this parking lot can get crowded and there may not be room for large RVs. There are campgrounds available. We stayed at the Wal-Mart one night going northbound and got a campground on the return trip.

Whitehorse is a small city, it's easy to get around, everything is relatively close, and (of course) they cater to tourists—RVers are definitely tourists. We discovered that if you go to the city administration building, they will give you (the tourist) a three-day parking pass. It's good at all parking meters and city parking lots and was really handy for us. This parking pass is not for your RV but for a normal vehicle.

On our return trip, we got a campground for five nights and were initially packed in tight with three caravans. The caravans pulled out the next morning so the place was mostly deserted. Much to our surprise, the park's cable TV brought in a few Seattle stations.

This was an unusual campground a short distance outside the city. They had a lower portion where they literally packed in the RVs. It was really tight side-to-side, no frills, and open to the sky—no trees on site. They also had an upper area (we drove up the hill and it was easy to maneuver) where the sites were private, treed, and quiet. Interestingly, almost no one was up there even though it was the same cost. As we found out later, they also had boondocking sites available, too. I do not know the cost, if any, for boondocking there.

There's lots of stuff to see in Whitehorse including several museums. Two unique things to see are the weathervane located at the Transportation (it used to be at the airport). The weathervane is a full-size DC-3 aircraft, mounted so that it turns and faces into the wind. Impressive!

They also have what is supposed to be the longest fish ladder in the world here. We visited it the first day but did not see any salmon (they have video under water). A fish ladder is designed to help the salmon move upstream more easily.

There are lots of things to see in the area. One of the unique sites is the *"Old Log Church."* It was actually a museum mostly focusing on religious history and artifacts. It was small and can be visited easily in one hour.

We both love any wild game —both to view it in the wild and to have it on the table. A deli (with the unique name of, *"The Deli"*) in Whitehorse was the consistent suggestion for lunch and we went. This was also the home of the *"Yukon Meat Company."* We had a great lunch and then purchased reindeer sausage and bison burger for dinner on the road later. We will eat this before we cross the USA border as I do not know if they will allow it across.

We also got tickets for the *"Frantic Follies"*—a vaudeville production that was fun and certainly entertaining. It took place in a small "showroom" in one of the hotels. It was definitely entertaining, fun for everyone, worthwhile, and a nice change for one evening. Sure enough, I am chosen to go up on stage (I get chosen all the time. I don't know why.) I don't want to be a spoilsport but would rather see the show than be in it! This show is a common stop for the caravans.

The *"Steamship Klondike"* was also a great tour. Owned by Parks Canada (their equivalent to our National Parks Service), they have a guided tour throughout the steamship. It was really well done. They have the vessel up, on land—no longer in the water— to help preserve it. This vessel was 230-

feet long and one of the largest ones on the Klondike River. It only required 6 feet of water to maneuver and was perfect for traveling the river. Our tour guide was knowledgeable and interesting. According to her, sailing on the Steamship Klondike was either first class or no class. If you could afford it, you didn't want no-class since this required you to sleep on or with whatever stores and supplies they were carrying.

We were just driving around in our car and followed the Yukon River as it meandered some distance out of Whitehorse. As expected, there are some spectacular views (see photo, p. 73).

We really enjoyed our time in Whitehorse. There were lots of things to see, a number of great places to eat, excellent places to visit, and it was easy to get around.

The Cassiar Highway

We pulled out of Whitehorse and headed east toward Watson Lake. Our next route, the Cassiar Highway, turns south about 12 miles (19 km) west of Watson Lake so we actually did not go all the way back into this tiny town.

There was an instant change in highway. The first 25 miles (40 km) or so was with the cruise control set at 35 mph (56 kph) with lots of 15–20 mph (24–32 kph) driving due to lots of gravel from lots of patching and resurfacing—sometimes several patches per mile! Some patches were lengthy but most were short stretches of gravel maybe four or five car-lengths long. The frequent short pieces of "good" (untouched) highway would not provide enough space/distance for you to pick up speed. We thought, oh well, it's only a 375-mile (604 km) drive to Stewart/Hyder!

We made it through the rough stuff and found that this highway is about one notch lower on my highway scale than the previous one. The Cassiar is two-lane, no guardrails, no shoulder, with 6–50-foot (1.8–15 meters) drop-offs, with occasional lane lines painted on the highway. The RCMP had a travel trailer stopped for some reason but since there was no shoulder, they simply took up the right lane. But, there was little or no traffic.

Notes on Driving the Cassiar Highway

What follows is more of a description of the drive and a few places to stay and see down the Cassiar Highway. Plus, I've included the second route (CA 37A)—the turn-off to Hyder/Stewart. This is due to the uniqueness of the Cassiar and surrounding wilderness, the lack of "tourist" places to stop, and the fact that there are virtually no towns on the route.

We thoroughly enjoyed the Cassiar and plan to drive it again. Do not let any seemingly negative statements deter you from taking this route. It's a great drive.

About 75 miles (120 km) down the Cassiar, we stopped at a tiny place called *"Jade City"* (two small buildings) to look at the jade. We learned they mine 75% of the world's jade here! There was a gift shop with many jade items and there were huge chunks of jade outside on display. We learned about the mining of jade. Interesting stuff!

Chatting with the workers, I asked where they bought their groceries (I did not see any other places to shop). They didn't bat an eye and simply said, "Watson Lake!" This means they have to drive 87 miles (140 km) **one way** to the grocery in a town of 1,200 (and drive over that construction described on the previous page)!

The good news is that Jade City has free overnight RV parking (boondocking). We didn't stay there but it looked nice enough.

We drove 120 miles (193 km) the first day on the Cassiar. Nice scenery—much like Yellowstone National Park —with a bit of snow on the mountains that are along the highway. We parked at a huge pull-off next to a beautiful lake and the loons were looning. Unfortunately, mosquitoes, too. For the last few days, they have come out —in droves. Open a window and 100 of them will be on the screen. Two or three seem to be getting in the coach at night— we must have a small hole somewhere.

At night, we spray the bedroom, close the door, then the bathroom, and close that door about an hour before we go to bed. Then, when we go to bed, we spray the front. This has helped. We thought of this as living with "Raid."

Route 37A or Turning West to Hyder/Stewart

Route 37A takes you off the Cassiar and turns toward the coast where the two towns of Hyder, Alaska and Stewart, BC are situated side-by-side.

Neither is a metropolis with Hyder at about 100 residents and Stewart about 500. This route is about 35 miles (56 km) long and is considered one of the most beautiful and spectacular in all of British Columbia—and that's saying a lot! The Bear Glacier, waterfalls, beaver dams, mountains, and streams mark your way. It is one great drive.

There was some road construction a short distance after we turned onto CA 37A but we still had plenty of space to pull off and take the photo of the Bear Glacier. Spectacular! Years ago, the glacier reached across to where we are parked. The construction of the highway could not be started until the glacier had melted back some.

Interestingly, this stretch of highway is good—even better than much of the Cassiar. My assumption is that it is maintained for the tourists (RVers).

This huge snow mass was impressive in August! It had to be from some earlier avalanche but whatever the source, it dropped a lot of snow and we had a great view from the highway!

Notice the small, black, cave-like hole in the bottom center of the snow. This is where the melted snow is actually running out into the stream. To help you gain a little perspective on the size of this giant pile, I could easily fit my coach inside this cave!

The ground here (in many places) is solid rock. So the drilling or placement of poles for electricity is virtually impossible or cost prohibitive. Rock is everywhere—big and small. They solved their power pole installation problem with the local rock. These piles were quite tall and some of the rocks were half the size of a car. It worked.

Hyder, Alaska

> **Author Note**: The reason Hyder information is presented here, not in the Alaska info but here at the end of Canadian Rt. 37A, is that Hyder is sort of stuck onto the side of Canada, at water's edge. You cannot pass through Stewart or Hyder by accident.

I've mentioned Hyder, Alaska several times throughout the book (p. 6, p. 17) but the main reason we came here is the bear viewing on Fish Creek. We have seen at least fifteen TV shows about how the bears catch the salmon to feed and we just wanted to see it. It's part of Alaska. So, we ended up in Hyder.

Just outside of Hyder, they have built a platform for viewing the bears and salmon. This is a built-up wooden, deck-like, 600-foot-long platform where tourists can walk out and see the grizzly bears catch and eat fish. You are protected from them. They are protected from you. It works.

It costs $5.00 to get in (access the platform) and is free with certain National Park Passes. There is usually a small crowd there every evening. The crowds will be larger if there are caravans in the area. You have to be patient, but the bears do show up. We saw several bears here one evening. Be sure and bring your camera.

Also, bring a tripod, too, if you have one. The best viewing is late evening and with the darker shadows, a tripod will help you capture some great shots of the bears. Your flash won't help—you will be too far away.

Remember at the beginning of the book, I explained that we didn't see any salmon during our trip (p. ix). Well, there weren't many here in Hyder either. Luckily, we saw a grizzly chase down one salmon and catch it. The bear spent some time on shore in front of us just eating away! Just like on TV. Fascinating.

All in all, we saw maybe 20 salmon. That's it, for the entire trip. It was the single negative thing on this great trip!

I've already mentioned that you must drive through Stewart, BC to get to Hyder and you must be aware that Hyder is pretty small. There are no paved roads in Hyder.

We stayed in Hyder at Camp Run-A-Muck (seriously—see p. 100). You have to understand, Hyder ain't all that exciting... we had a drink in the only bar in town and then ate at the only restaurant in town.

> **Author Note**: We were told that there used to be two restaurants in Hyder but the cook from the "other" restaurant was taking a motorcycle trip and their kitchen was closed (seriously). There may be two when you go there.

The only remaining restaurant was named *"The Bus"* because the woman who runs it (her husband is a fisherman) cooks in an old school bus (seriously) and then brings the food out the door. There were two seating areas—outside on the picnic tables and inside an empty garage also on picnic tables. We both had fish and chips. The fresh halibut was wonderful. It's amazing what you can do in a school bus.

We were also told there were only two steady, fulltime jobs in Hyder—one, the postmaster and the other was the teacher. The Post Office is a mobile home. We didn't see the school.

Hyder, Alaska is so close to Stewart, BC, that the only clock in town on official Alaskan time is located at the post office. Everything else sort of normally functions on Pacific time (one hour earlier) to match up with Stewart. It may not be a perfect system but it works. For the RVers who like to eat later, don't forget this time difference if you are going to go out to a restaurant in Stewart.

If you want to have your mail forwarded to Hyder, note that it arrives via float plane on Mondays and Thursdays. If the plane doesn't arrive (for whatever reason), there is no mail delivery so you will have to wait at least a day. If you can't stay around Hyder, leave your forwarding address with the postmaster. He is very accommodating in forwarding your mail to another U.S. post office.

We spent almost no time in Stewart even though it is the first tiny town you come to going west on 37A. Laid out in a grid, it is easy to get through. You will see a couple of restaurants and gift shops while driving through. If you are a serious shopper or browser, this is not going to be your best day—sorry.

Stewart also has a free dump station fully accessible to all. It is easy to get to, plenty of room to maneuver the biggest rig, and was clean. I believe there was potable water available, too. We didn't need it so I'm just not sure.

Still heading south, we left Hyder after two nights. It's about 475 miles (764 km) to Prince George and we spent three nights on the road getting there.

Alaskan Info

Although at first, it may seem strange that Alaska is very different in many ways from the "Lower 48." However, it truly makes sense when you study their location. They are connected to Canada—nothing else. Up there, you cannot drive from state-to-state so they are a standalone.

In many cases, they make—and follow—their own rules. For example, I know of no other state where you can just pull off the road—virtually anywhere—and spend the night (more on this later).

Alaska is a huge state. The standard joke used to be that if they cut Alaska in half, Texas would be the third largest state. Now you hear that when the tide is out, they could cut

Alaska into thirds and Texas would be the fourth largest state! They can say this because Alaska has more coastline than the rest of the United States combined!

Yes, Alaska is big, but not driving-accessible for the most part. There are a few highways, most all of them paved (except for ongoing repair), and are well maintained. These highways go to various towns and the two "cities" up there. There are only three cities with over 10,000 population. Anchorage is, of course, the largest at about 250,000. But the other two—Fairbanks and Juneau (the state capitol)—are just over 30,000 each. However, you cannot drive to Juneau. It is only accessible by boat or air. (For you trivia buffs, it is the only state capitol not accessible by car.)

People fly everywhere in Alaska. The use of small airplanes is common to cross the state. Interestingly, since many of the companies that built small airplanes went out of business years ago, the planes are rebuilt—over and over. It is not unusual to get into a plane originally manufactured in the 1950s or 1960s!

Sea (float) planes (normal planes fitted with pontoons for water landings) are the common method of getting around since there are lakes and rivers everywhere. We have all heard about Minnesota being the "Land of 10,000 lakes." However, Alaska estimates that it has over 3,000,000 (that's three million) lakes! So for hunting, fishing, or just getting away from it all, the easy and common method is to fly in and land on the water.

These same planes are also used in the winter. However, they do trade the pontoons for skis. This allows the planes to land on snow-covered runways or other surfaces.

Notice the skis mounted under the wheels. These allow the pilot to land on any relatively level, snow-covered surface. Here, we landed on a glacier as part of our "flightseeing" tour out of Talkeetna and around Denali (the park and the mountain).

Alaska is on "Alaskan" time (a real time zone) that is one hour later than Pacific time. So, tell your east coast friends not to call you during their morning coffee as there is a four-hour difference! Remember, 8:00 AM on the east coast is just 4:00 AM in Alaska! The sun may be up but you likely won't be.

We ran across the ubiquitous "coupon book" for sale in Alaska and actually ended up with one. The book was donated to us by the company that sold it.

We found that we did not use the book (maybe one time). However, I have talked with many RVers that did purchase them and said they definitely got their money's worth. Check carefully. If it works for you, do it.

Highways in Alaska

Although they exist, Alaskans do not use major route or highway numbers such as AK-1 or AK-3. Even through Canada, the highway numbers are not often used on the main routes going to Alaska. If you ask a local about how to get to AK-3, they may not know what you are talking about.

They have names for the various routes/highways. For example, AK-1 is the Sterling Highway and AK-3 is the Parks Highway. Again, in Canada, Route 97 up through British Columbia and the continuation through the Yukon Territory (Route 1) is simply called the Alaska Highway (this is the old ALCAN Highway). The guidebooks, brochures, websites, and local people will all use the names. You will have to learn them. All "official" government maps will show the route numbers but may not show the names. Be sure to check for both names and numbers.

Where to Pull Off

You will want to pull off anyway to appreciate the scenery. This picture of the waterfall is a pull-off just a bit north of Valdez. It was paved and there was room for numerous full-sized RVs. Plus, there was a second waterfall just as large as this one!

According to the Alaskan State Trooper main information

number, it is legal to pull off the highway and spend the night. The main criteria are that you must be at least 4-feet from the solid white line, must leave room for an additional vehicle, and of course, don't dump anything.

There are pull-offs and "official" rest areas everywhere—Alaska has more than I've seen anywhere else including Canada and the "Lower 48." I have seen as many as three per mile in some areas of the state and they were all nice and large. That's great for two reasons. First, it is illegal to block more than five vehicles driving behind you. Pull off and let them pass. The locals will appreciate it and some tourists (most likely RVers?) may be in a hurry.

Second, you will have the opportunity to spend the night with some spectacular scenery and maybe be visited

by an occasional animal. We stayed overnight at Willow Lake (see above) on our way from Tok to Valdez. We spent the night alone, in a huge pull-off, parked by the edge of the grass, overlooking the lake, listening to the sounds of nature.

Campgrounds in Alaska

Campgrounds are mostly 30-amp, many do not have sewer hook-ups at the site, a few have cable TV (often with only 2-3-4 pretty snowy channels), and our average cost was in the mid-to-high $30.00 range in 2008.

For current and accurate information on campgrounds for your Alaskan trip, get a copy of *Traveler's Guide to Alaskan Camping* by Mike and Terri Church (see p. 27).

I can't and won't comment on all the campgrounds we stayed in. However, some stand out for various reasons. One of those—Camp Run-A-Muck (seriously)—was in Hyder, Alaska (read more about Hyder, p. 90).

When we arrived, Camp Run-A-Muck was busy with a caravan, had 30-amp, water, with just a few sewer-hook-up sites on a septic system. We were situated on a gravel site next to a gravel road. It could get dusty with traffic.

The manager asked if we could manage without sewer and we said sure. The manager said their campground had an agreement with the town of Stewart so we could dump there on our way out. Everything worked out fine.

They had a book exchange at the campground office where you could trade in your tired old books. It was strictly on the honor system.

This is Not a Travelogue

While I could continue to write extensively about the great places to visit in Alaska, the information that follows will identify a few good ones—especially for your first RV trip. There are many others and my not including them here is not, in any way, an indication of their quality. The cities of Anchorage and Fairbanks have great, sites, tours, museums, parks, and unique places to visit. Other towns are equally worthwhile. Stop and stay a few days. Talk to the locals. You will thoroughly enjoy your time there. Alaskans are casual, enjoy life, and like to joke with the numerous visitors to their great state.

This is my "list" of places to visit from one trip, one time. We saw lots of things but also missed out on many places. We did what we could in the time that we had. And we had a great time.

So my group of places is primarily where we went. I certainly recommend them to you but if you find others, let me know. I'll visit different ones on the next trip and many of these same ones again.

I have never been a tour guide but we are constantly asked for recommendations. We do this same asking about places we have never visited so the cycle repeats itself. How else do you find information and get help? Guidebooks and the Internet are good but a first-hand description is hard to beat. In the next chapter, I describe a few places to visit and there are many, many others.

We only planned two scheduled "events" during our RV trip. Everything else was spur of the moment. The two events were the Alaska Samboree in Palmer and the Moose Dropping Festival in Talkeetna.

10:30 at night. There was plenty of sunshine when we were there. We used polar fleece and made "blackout" curtains for the bedroom. Otherwise, it was too bright to sleep.

Alaska Samboree

The Alaska Samboree, like in other states, is held once per year and it was pure coincidence that we were going to be in the same location at the same time. This Samboree was held in June at the Alaska State Fairgrounds in Palmer, just east of Anchorage. We knew we were going to be leaving Anchorage just about the time the Alaska Samboree started and, since Palmer is only about 30 miles (48 km) to Anchorage, we decided to go.

The Samboree committee gave us the go-ahead to present a few of our seminars. So, we did. It was a pleasant experience. One major advantage was that we met a number of Alaskan RVers (locals, not tourists) and they gave us good advice about the remainder of our trip.

Moose Dropping Festival

The Moose Dropping Festival is held mid-July in Talkeetna—a small town (pop. 850) north of Anchorage. For you TV trivia/sitcom fans, it was rumored that Talkeetna was the model for that wacky show on several years ago called "Northern Exposure" but I can't verify that.

I can verify that they do not actually drop a moose for any part of the festival. What does happen is that before the festival weekend, the local residents go into the woods, pick up moose droppings (yes, those real manure "pellets"), bring them back, paint them white, and number each one. I think there were about 1,500 of these numbered pellets. During the festival (there are lots of people who come to Talkeetna for this), locals will sell you an official, numbered, moose-dropping pellet (painted white). You are given a pellet with a unique number on it and a corresponding, numbered pellet goes into the big bag.

The climax to the three-day festival is when they raise the big bag way up in the air and then drop the bag of pellets onto a hard surface (concrete). There is an "X" painted on the concrete and the pellet landing closest to the "X" wins a money prize. There are other money prizes and some (my guess) goes to charity or maybe next year's event.

You will find it common for the locals to refer to the moose droppings as "mooseberries." Many individuals also decorate their personal "moose" (as shown here) and set them out for all to see. It's all in fun, the shops are open, food and drink is available, and no moose were harmed during the event. That's good.

There were maybe a dozen decorated "moose" all over town. Each was customized to represent their respective sponsor. Notice the bandaged leg and the crutch. This one was sponsored by a local doctor.

Be A Tourist

We are good tourists (it's what we do) and Alaska is a great place to be one. You have constant and spectacular sights around you while the man-made history is intriguing, unique, and interesting. We panned for gold (got some, too).

We learned about the history of the gold strikes and how they get it today. Interesting stuff. From the pipeline to earthquakes to dogsleds to fishing to glaciers, Alaska has a relatively brief, self-generated, history that was influenced from within, not from neighboring states (there are none) or the country next door.

Alaskan history is very different from that of the "Lower 48." Alaska was originally settled by various tribes of what is now referred to as "Alaska Natives." (This is distinctly different from the term "Native Alaskan," referring to anyone born in Alaska.) The ancestors of Alaska Natives apparently walked across the land-bridge connecting Alaska from what we now know as Russia. That land-bridge no longer exists and is now under the Bering Sea.

Russian fur traders established the first toe-hold on Kodiak Island and then, about 1795, established a trading post near Sitka. Throughout the early 1800s, Russia was trying to colonize Alaska and at one point, it is estimated that the Russian population reached 700—a large number of people at that time.

There was a strong desire by the Russians to keep Alaska out of British hands. That, plus low profits from trade with Alaskan settlements and serious financial difficulties within Russia all contributed to Russia's willingness to sell its various possessions in North America. The primary effort to complete this purchase was led by U.S. Secretary of State

William Seward. On April 9, 1867, the United States Senate approved the purchase of Alaska from Russia for $7.2 million. At the time, this purchase was commonly called "Seward's Folly" or "Seward's Icebox" in the media (newspapers) and was unpopular with the general populace. It was later, that the discovery of gold and oil would verify the purchase to be a worthwhile one.

We visited many small museums in the various towns and I recommend them all. Each had a slightly different focus, none were large, some charged a small fee, others asked for a donation, many were free, and all of them provided a better understanding of the local area and the state in general. Don't miss these. They are the history and heart of Alaska in small doses.

Some Alaskan Places to Go

We have had the good fortune to visit Alaska on four occasions (actually, five for me). Three of those visits were on a Princess cruise ship. We are avid cruisers and have been on many. The major trip, of course, was in the RV.

My first very brief (about three hours) visit was on my way back from Vietnam. We landed in Anchorage and were confined to a bar in the airport (seriously). What got my attention was flying in and out. Flying over those rugged, snow-capped mountains really stuck in my memory and, although it took years, I couldn't wait to return there and see Alaska first hand. It was worth it.

What follows is a brief overview of what we did on our RV trip to Alaska. We did not go everywhere and never planned to try to do it all in one trip. It's too big. I had plans to go back even before we got there—but that's just me.

We did try to cover the well-known places, stay as long as we wanted in any one place, took numerous side trips in our car, took paid tours, and were good tourists. The places are listed in the order we visited them. Not every attraction is listed for every town—primarily the ones we visited but some others, too.

Valdez

We spent a week here at the Eagle's Rest Campground. It was just fine. There are plenty of good restaurants in Valdez and we hit them all (well, most of them). Fresh halibut is on every menu. Be sure to walk down on the docks when the fishing charters come in. They clean the fish right there and you can watch. Some of those giant halibut are pretty impressive. I recommend at least three museums...

- **Valdez Museum & Historical Archive...** local history, native culture, gold rush, oil spill, and a summer quilt exhibit. <www.valdezmuseum.org>

- **Remembering Old Valdez Exhibit 1957–1967...** We learned the details of the 1964 Good Friday Earthquake. Because of that earthquake and the resulting damage, they decided to move the entire town of Valdez a couple of miles away from it's original location. It's a fascinating history of living and eking out a living in a rugged land.

- **Whitney Museum...** native art, ivory carving, and wildlife mounts. Located at the Prince William Sound Community College. <www.uaa.alaska.edu/pwscc>

There are fine campgrounds in Valdez but you can move your RV across the bay to a boondocking site close to the oil terminal. Owned by the city, there is a nightly charge but the cost is minimal. We even found drinking water there provided by the city. There is a fish hatchery close to here where salmon get up the creek using a fish ladder.

There are two local Valdez glaciers. One, the **Worthington Glacier**, has a large parking lot, walkways, and viewing platform at the base of the glacier near the road. Exit at Mile 28.7, Richardson Highway, just outside Valdez. Visit the interpretive viewing shelter, hike the one-mile Moraine Trail close to the blue ice, explore cracks and pools at the glacier terminus—but *stay off the ice*. Climb the Ridge Trail to explore alpine tundra, more hanging glaciers, and a spectacular view of the valley.

The snout of the **Valdez Glacier** is relatively flat and makes for an easy walk. It is located on the outskirts of Valdez and is full of Alaskan history. It was called the "All American Route" by gold seekers wanting to trek over the glacier into the interior of Alaska during the Gold Rush of 1898. The area around the glacier has many trails.

Whittier

The ferry from Valdez to Whittier saved us miles and time plus lots of backtracking. The scenery would be spectacular but we thought the ferry would also offer unique sights, too. It did. We were not disappointed.

To drive in or out of Whittier, there is a 2.5-mile (4 km) one-way tunnel—a unique drive! They took the working railroad tunnel, filled in along the tracks, and you actually drive the tracks —like a streetcar route. Cars are released each direction on the half-hour. Trains have priority. The tunnel may seem a bit narrow for your RV (but it's big enough for the train). It works.

The Kenai Peninsula

Alaska is made up of various geographical areas—only a few of which are accessible by RV. One of the most popular is the Kenai Peninsula. This is the southern land mass (a very large peninsula) that sits due south of Anchorage and northwest of the Inside Passage (the route where the cruise ships travel).

A little larger than Maryland, most of the Kenai is inaccessible by road because it is nearly covered by two national parks. There are two major highways and within about three hours driving, you can be in the town of Homer —on the extreme southern tip of the Kenai. RVers from the Anchorage area verify that fact every summer weekend. It can get a bit busy but there is lots of room. Coming up from the "Lower 48," you won't be limited to the weekends so plan for at least two or three weeks on the Kenai—longer is okay, too.

Homer

Perched on the southern tip of the Kenai, the city of Homer (pop. 5,400) is an RV-friendly community. Billed as the "Halibut Capital of the World," Homer has fishing charters everywhere.

The Homer Spit is a 4–5 mile-long (7 km) narrow stretch of land in Kachemak Bay—a huge body of salt water surrounded by snow-capped mountains. There are at least three private campgrounds on the Spit. Every site has a great (or slightly obstructed) view of the mountains and bay.

The city also operates three large dry-camping areas (no hookups) on the Spit. Pull in, sign up, put your $15.00/day in the "Iron Ranger" (the metal container), find a spot, park your coach, life is good, and the view is better. You are within walking distance of restaurants, bars, shops, and, of course, fishing charters. There's a two-week maximum stay. There is plenty of room on the Spit for your motorhome even if you just want to park and have dinner.

For a real treat, find Skyline Drive (in Homer) and start at the northern end. Meander this for impressive views of Homer, the Spit, and the bay. Skyline Drive is very steep at one end so don't take the big rig. For Class C drivers, you will have to come down in a low gear. My estimate is the south end of Skyline Drive was at least a 12% grade.

The **"Oceans and Islands Visitor's Center"** in Homer is one of the most unique in Alaska. It is located on the main highway going through the town headed for the Spit. They created huge dioramas inside showing the coastal regions and various wildlife. It is really well done—don't miss it. Unfortunately, there is limited parking at this Visitor Center. Don't try to go in there with your big rig. Locate your campsite first, park the RV, set up, and come back. You will have to spend an hour or so to see everything in this place.

Pratt Museum

This is a "don't miss." You will learn about the history and cultures that have inhabited the Kachemak Bay area (that huge body of water seen in the previous photo). They have two distinct fascinating projects.

One is Oral History. The following is from their website:

"The things that give our lives a distinct local flavor are the climate, the resources, the view, and our remoteness. Just about everyone owns rubber boots, a skiff, and a car with character. We wear spikes on our shoes in the winter and long johns in the summer. We eat more ice cream than any people anywhere. Hair is valued more for warmth than looks. And, if you don't smell like fish, you're probably not from around here. All of us are tied to living in this place and sustaining our unique regional lifestyle."

Second is their "Wild Video Cameras." They have cameras set up in remote locations. You can view Alaskan Seabirds on Gull Island and view the bears feeding at Brooks Falls in the Katmai National Park.

<www.prattmuseum.org>

Soldotna

Leaving Homer on Sterling Highway (AK-1), we had a leisurely drive north along the Cook Inlet about 75 miles (120 km) to Soldotna (pop. 3,800). This is a nice drive with many places to pull off the highway. Most pull-offs would easily accommodate a large motorhome. There are limited services in a few tiny towns so we fueled up in Homer.

Think fish! Soldotna was voted the #1 Fishing Hotspot in North America by Field & Stream Magazine in 2004. The Kenai River flows through the town and offers world-class Chinook (King), Sockeye (Red), Coho (Silver), and Pink

Salmon fishing. Downtown has a 3,700-foot-long elevated fishing boardwalk along the Kenai River for all to enjoy. People use the boardwalk for a stroll as well as fishing.

We boondocked the first night in Soldotna at an unusual location that had free Wi-Fi. It was behind a laundromat. I had heard about this place, searched Google for laundromats, started calling, and found one that told me to come on in. It worked just fine plus we did a massive laundry, too! You could also overnight at the Soldotna Fred Meyer grocery with lots of other RVs. Call or go in and ask. They had a dump site, too. If you need to hook up, local campgrounds offer RVers over 200 private campsites as well.

With plenty of space for big RV parking, Soldotna is famous for the *"Moose is Loose Bakery!"* They had special glazed and chocolate-covered donuts—each one would barely fit on a normal dinner plate! Seriously! They had also taken normal cinnamon rolls, "flattened" them so they were about 8 x 12 inches (and thin), and baked them crispy. They were affectionately called "Road Kill Caramel Rolls!"

With luck, you may be able to drive the big rig out the rear of the Bakery parking lot. Sometimes it is blocked.

Seward

This is a great town located on the eastern coast of the Kenai. As we have identified in the following pages, there is lots of touristy stuff to do here.

They even bring some cruise ships into Seward and the place can get crowded. The ships are easy to spot and you can actually stay away from that crowd as there are plenty of places to eat, drink, and tour in the downtown area.

Seward Museum

This small, interesting museum takes you through Seward's history with photographs, artifacts, and documents plus a collection of Native baskets and ivory carvings. During summer, they have presented evening programs consisting of two slide/tape shows entitled *"The History of Seward"* and *"The History of the Iditarod Trail."* A special open house is held every August 28th in honor of the founding of Seward in 1903.

Alaska SeaLife Center

The Alaska SeaLife Center is the only project in the state authorized to capture and rehabilitate animals. We took a behind-the-scenes tour that was excellent and spent time feeding the birds, learning how they take care of them, and what they do with the data collected. The puffins were wonderful and impressive up close!

The Center is a large, modern building and current research/rehabilitation work is serious. You can visit the

Center without the extra behind-the-scenes tour but I recommend seeing it all.
<www.alaskasealife.org>

Kenai Fjords National Park

Seward is on the edge of the Kenai Fjords National Park. You cannot take your motorhome through the park so they operate half-day and day-long boat tours. The boat tour is a must-do and will be one of the highlights of your visit. I recommend the day-long trip. Our boat tour found several whales, sea lions, eagles, and other wildlife throughout the day-long venture.

We also saw several glaciers and sailed very close to one of them—close enough to easily hear the glacier groaning, cracking, and creaking as it constantly moved. We were lucky

enough to see it "calve" several times and watched giant chunks of ice breaking away, falling, and creating a massive splash. An impressive sight! On the return trip, we stopped at a lodge (on Fox Island) for a grilled salmon dinner. It was absolutely excellent.

Exit Glacier… is in the only part of the Kenai Fjords National Park accessible by road. Drive in and you can walk the trails very close to the active glacier. Ranger-led walk are also available.

To get there, exit Glacier Road at Mile 3 on the Seward Highway. The 8.6 mile road to the Exit Glacier Area is paved. Take your car, not your big motorhome. The Kenai Fjords National Park is one of only three national parks in Alaska that can be reached by road

The Iditarod

From Anchorage, in south central Alaska, to Nome on the western Bering Sea coast, each team of 12–16 dogs and their musher cover over 1,150 miles (1,850 km) in 10–17 days.

The original start of the dogsled race—named the Iditarod—was in Seward. Currently, there is a commemorative start in Anchorage plus a "restart" in Wasilla—west of Anchorage. (Note: In 2008, Wasilla gained international fame because Sarah Palin was mayor here before her election as Governor of Alaska.)

The Iditarod Trail, now a National Historic Trail, had its beginnings as a mail and supply route from the coastal towns of Seward and Knik to the interior mining camps at Flat, Ophir, Ruby and beyond to the west coast communities of Unalakleet, Elim, Golovin, White Mountain, and Nome. Mail and supplies went in. Gold came out—all via dog sled. Heroes were made and legends were born.

The origins of the race are based on a dogsled run in 1925 when part of the Iditarod Trail became a life-saving highway for epidemic-stricken Nome. Diphtheria threatened and serum had to be brought in, again by dog mushers and their faithful hard-driving dogs.

North of the Kenai

Leaving the Kenai is easy. You drive the one highway (Seward Highway) or take a ferry, period. Driving, your first major stop is Anchorage but there are a few towns along the way. To get to Anchorage, you must drive along one side of a major body of water called Turnagain Arm. This is a pleasant drive and there are several pull-offs almost at water's edge. The bore tide in Turnagain Arm is a once-in-a-lifetime viewing when it occurs.

Going to Palmer (a short drive east of Anchorage), you enter the Matanuska Valley—the "growing region" known for its abundance and huge vegetables. With the short season, long days, and a fine mix of glacial silt and loam, vegetables grow rapidly to an unbelievable—even giant—size in this flood plain. Try to visualize broccoli 3-feet tall with a 7-foot-wide head, 98-pound cabbages, and 25-pound mushrooms. We were here the end of June and it was too early for us to see any but they show the veggies here at the State Fair in August.

Reindeer Farm

The reindeer and caribou are the same animal. They are called caribou in the wild and reindeer in captivity. Here at the Reindeer Farm you can meander among a small herd and feed them. <www.reindeerfarm.com>

Musk Ox Farm

This huge (1,000+ pounds) animal is one ugly dude with two claims to fame. First, they shed "Qiviut," one of the finest, softest, and most expensive "wools."

How expensive? One ball of Qiviut (equal to a ball of yarn) was $90.00! It's woven just like yarn but is eight times warmer than sheep's wool, lighter weight, and won't shrink.

Second, the musk ox is unique as the northernmost species of hoofed animal in the world. They can live and survive very comfortably in –70° (that's 70-BELOW-zero) weather. Excellent tour.
<www.muskoxfarm.org>

Anchorage

This is a major city (pop. 250,000) and you can expect some crowds, lots of traffic, stop lights, crosswalks, and tourists—lots of tourists. There were an unlimited number of shops (large and small), tourist-type places, and of course, plenty of tee-shirts for sale. With all that, we found Anchorage to be clean and bright and easy to get around while driving. There were large hanging baskets of flowers hanging on every street corner—well kept and blooming. The people are friendly. There are a gazillion restaurants for you to try and most were the non-chain variety.

Anchorage is bordered by two military installations—Fort Richardson (Army) and Elmendorf AFB (Air Force). The two installations actually share a common border. We were told that they would be combined as a cost-cutting measure and this work was underway.

Notes for Military People

If you have ID card privileges (you know who you are), Elmendorf AFB and Fort Richardson both have FamCamps. Both are on gravel and in the trees. If possible, drive your car to both (they are pretty close together) and check them out before you make a decision. The Fort Richardson FamCamp also had a book exchange.

Elmendorf AFB has a mess hall *open to everyone with base-access privileges*. (Access is allowed at the discretion of the Base

Commander and can change depending on mission and security issues. Sometimes the base hosts special exercises and they limit non-active duty access.) The "Iditarod Dining Facility" is a "food court" type of eatery where you can order what you want. It's a fairly new facility and the food was excellent and inexpensive. They do not serve alcohol.

Ship Creek State Hatchery

Yes, you can view salmon (if they are running) in Anchorage. Drive to just outside the entrance to Elmendorf AFB (marked "Gate 3") to "Ship Creek." You will need to take the short walk through the open gate. There is also a fish ladder there. When we were there, you had to walk through where the fence was pushed down to actually get back to the stream.

Alaska Aviation Heritage Museum

Alaska's unique aviation history, bush pilots who opened up the Last Frontier, rare aircraft photographs, artifacts, maps, news accounts, films, and aviators' clothing make this place unique. You simply could not survive in Alaska without the bush pilots. <www.alaskaairmuseum.com>

Anchorage Museum

Close to downtown, this museum contains galleries of art, native artifacts, and full-sized replicas of native dwellings. It is a busy stop because virtually all the tours stop here. <www.anchoragemuseum.org>

Anchorage Farmer's Market

During 2009, the market was located at 15th & Cordova and is the only non-profit, farmer-directed market in Anchorage. It was open from 9:00 AM to 2:00 PM on Saturday, only. They sell locally-grown produce, organic vegetables, cheddar cheese, cheese curds, ice cream, and a variety of trinkets. It's definitely worth a visit.
<www.anchoragefarmersmarket.org>

Denali National Park

Completion of the Parks Highway created a direct route to Denali park. Officials implemented a mass transit system in the park beyond Mile 15 on the Denali Park Road.

This is the only road in the park, and with few exceptions, private vehicles are not allowed. The Denali Park Road extends 91 miles (146 km) from the entrance to the old mining community of Kantishna. It is mostly gravel, crossing forests and sub-arctic tundra, mountainsides, sheer cliffs, and prime wildlife viewing areas.

There are commercial campgrounds on the Park Highway near the entrance to the park. Denali National Park and Preserve has seven campgrounds and three are available for RVers…

- Riley Creek, 1/4 mile (0.4 km) from Park Entrance
- Savage River, 13 miles (21 km)
- Teklanika River, 29 miles (47 km).

There is a three-night minimum stay at Teklanika River. There are no gas stations or services west of the Denali Park Hotel and no telephones west of Park Headquarters. Please leave towed vehicles in the Riley Creek overflow parking lot.

To reduce road traffic, *your road pass is good only for one trip into the campground and one trip out*. Make sure you use the RV dump station at Riley Creek Campground and buy all necessary items before going to Teklanika. Once at the campground, you may not return temporarily to headquarters. Transportation back to the campground is unavailable unless you purchased a camper bus ticket. You may camp a total of 14 days in Park Service campgrounds.

RVers must follow the detailed regulation and policies to camp in the Park, e.g., there are unusual "rules" for generator usage. Start with this website...
<www.denali.national-park.com/camping.htm>

To reduce traffic congestion and protect the natural resources of the park, bus tours are offered daily. Drivers are knowledgeable and efficient. It is a great way to see the Park. There are different bus options and tour lengths. One of the advantages of taking the bus is that the drivers know where much of the wildlife feeds and lingers and will point this out to your group. Plus, they stop, you can get off, stretch, and take your pictures.

Fairbanks

This is the second major city in Alaska (pop. 35,000+) and the northernmost stop for most tourists—like RVers. You can go farther north of Fairbanks—for another 500± miles (805± km)—but most choose not to. We personally enjoyed Fairbanks a bit better than Anchorage but only because we like cities about this size. There were ample restaurants and tourist sites plus it was easy to get around in our car.

There are a number of activities and places to visit in and around (but close to) Fairbanks. On our route, Fairbanks was the last city northbound. We headed south from here toward (and through) North Pole, Delta Junction, and ultimately back to Tok. However, we stayed a week in Fairbanks and had a great visit.

Fairbanks Visitor Center

> Like many Visitor Centers, this place is the place to start your visit to the Fairbanks area. They have a wealth of information online and will mail you lots of other stuff. The website is operated by The Fairbanks Convention and Visitors Bureau with lots of information to help you find your way around.
> <www.explorefairbanks.com>

University of Alaska Museum of the North

> This large museum is located on the University of Alaska Fairbanks campus. There is visitor

> parking available for recreational vehicles adjacent to the museum and summer hours were extended from 9:00 AM to 9:00 PM. Check as this could easily change.

The UofA "Museum" houses a nice variety of collections—all with a focus on Alaskan history and culture. It is a rich collection and worth your time.

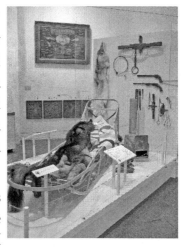

You cannot see this museum in a quickie walk-through visit. I recommend you allocate at least 4–5 hours to enjoy the sights (just take another look at the size of the building on the previous photo). So I recommend you plan to spend a long half-day here. It will be worth it! Just to see their collection and display of gold (nuggets, dust, and jewelry) is worth the effort! <www.uaf.edu/museum/>

Alaskan Pipeline

We learned all about the Alaskan Pipeline. We had never seen it before but many of you will recall when it dominated our daily news about 40 years ago. It was a big deal then and is equally fascinating today.

The history of the pipeline was presented in various museums. However, there are sites where you could drive in, park, walk around, and actually touch the pipeline (It's warm, supposedly from the oil flowing through it.). We learned that the first barrel of oil didn't flow though the pipeline but was hauled by dogsled to Valdez.

Author Note: Although the pipeline was not specific to only Fairbanks, just north of the city was one of the better access points (as shown above).

Fairbanks Ice Museum

See a movie and meander through some of the actual ice carvings from the World Ice Art Championships. Take a jacket as you will have the opportunity to walk in the giant freezers and get up close and personal with the huge ice carvings. Plus, they will do an actual ice-carving demonstration for you. This place is in the heart of the city and there is only street parking. Do not drive your big rig there. <www.icemuseum.com>

Summer Solstice Celebration

Also known as "Midnight Sun Events," this celebration begins the third week in June. On June 21, the actual solstice marks the halfway point for summer and the beginning of their descent into another winter. They use this time to celebrate warm weather while they can.

A pilgrimage of sorts takes place to Eagle Summit, 107 miles (172 km) up the Steese Highway. "A combination picnic, camp out, and tailgate party" the News-Miner calls the small, impromptu, informal party held every year on a mountain top north of Fairbanks. It is a good place to set up your camera and tripod to take multiple exposures as the sun moves slowly across the horizon, never quite touching the Crazy Mountains in the distance. It's one of those local "things" that are unique and fun.

For those choosing not to make the photo trip, the Midnight Sun Festival also takes place in the city. They celebrate the longest day of the year with music, shopping, crafts, special entertainment, and a downtown street fair. Many stores stay open until midnight. <http://fairbanks-alaska.com>

Midnight Sun Baseball Game

Scheduled for June 21st, the Alaska Goldpanners baseball team begins its widely acclaimed contest **without artificial lighting**. The *"high noon at midnight"* classic is an annual ritual on the longest day of the year.

Gold Dredge No. 8

A unique tour of Alaska's industrial mining history. You can actually walk through the giant dredge. <www.golddredgeno8.com>

El Dorado Gold Mine

We got an excellent demonstration of sluice-box gold mining plus you also get to pan for gold. We found some. Actually, they guarantee you will find some. You also get to keep what you find. <www.eldoradogoldmine.com>

Riverboat Discovery

The riverboat departs from the edge of Fairbanks for a 3.5 hour cruise on the Chena River. You will visit the home and pass Trail Breaker kennels of the late, four-time Iditarod champion Susan Butcher. Plus, there is a tour of a Chena Indian Village. <riverboatdiscovery.com>

Creamer's Field Migratory Waterfowl Refuge

Friends of Creamer's Field is a community based nonprofit organization dedicated to historical preservation and natural history education at Creamer's Field Migratory Waterfowl Refuge, Fairbanks, Alaska. Friends of Creamer's Field operates in cooperation with the Alaska Department of Fish and Game. Meander the forest, wetlands, ponds, and open fields. <www.fairnet.org/agencies/creamers>

We Learned Something and Had Fun

You have to know that there is **a lot more to see** on this trip than what I listed here. Plus, my list may not match your list—but that's okay. I never intended to see it all or even try to see it all. I plan to go back.

When we visit what I call the "tourist" places (and I do not mean this as a derogatory term), Sandy and I generally try to take it all in. We look, read extensively, talk to the people, take any guided tours (paid or free), and take our time. We want to see it. It's what we do.

Say Bye-Bye

As with all trips, this one must come to an end, too. Eighty-four days after we crossed that US/Canadian border headed northbound, we crossed it again—this time heading south. Our return border crossing was in Blaine, Washington. Blaine has the notoriety of being the northernmost town in the continental United States and sits directly south of Vancouver, BC.

We spent a few days in Vancouver and then crossed over. Blaine is a busy crossing with lots of traffic and the lanes are confusing. Due to some conflicting signage, getting in the correct lane was somewhat of a challenge. I actually did not know if I was in the correct lane until I reached the guard booth. It turned out okay but as most of you are aware, you cannot back up a motorhome when you are towing a car. So, we did our best to figure it out and then took our chances with the best guess. Somehow, it worked and we were fine.

Since we fulltime (and have for about seven years), I used this border crossing as the "end" of the our Alaskan trip. (After all, we just kept going and meandered down the west coast to San Diego and then headed for Texas.) My mileage for the trip was 13,000± (20,921 km) but remember, I did not go directly back to my starting point (Dallas, Texas).

My Focus

It was my goal to find and furnish you with enough current information, facts, data, and in some cases, speculation about what to do to help you initially discuss, plan for, start, and complete an Alaskan trip. I talked with a large number of people about this—some were RVers and some were not. I have included many websites. I have no idea if these will still be valid, working sites when you try them and, of course, have no control over their quality. My decision to include them was simply based on the fact that if some of them do work for you, they will have some valuable, useful information. Good luck.

For those of you that do try it, you have my best wishes and a sincere "Good Luck" in your efforts. Remember, I'm here to help and know a lot of resources where you can get help. So, if you have a question, comment, complaint, or just want to say hello, here's my e-mail address. Don't hesitate to send me a note at…

alaska@aboutrving.com

Thanks for reading this far.

I hope this collection of information helps.

Let me know if it does and let me know if it doesn't.

R. E. Jones

Author Note: It was a pleasure writing this book because it allowed me to relive this fantastic trip again and again.

Early June 2010, we will be driving the Cassiar Highway northbound, going to Skagway, and with the car only, take the ferry to Sitka. When we return, we drive south on the Cassiar to Prince Rupert, B.C. There, we put the motorhome on the ferry to Port Hardy (the north end of Vancouver Island). We will meander down island for a couple of weeks.

If you want to be included on my mail list for announcements or updates, please e-mail me at...
        alaska@aboutrving.com

Thanks for reading this far.

                                      Ron Jones

Try these, too...

They make *great* gifts!

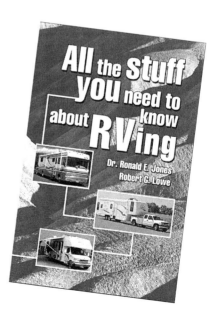

Order online at...
aboutrving.com

Questions? Call...
800-262-3060

A whole new website!

aboutrving.com

Welcome to the only true "How To" site for RVers. Sure, there are thousands of other sites but we have organized ours so you can easily find the help you need in one place for nearly all things RV and all types of RVs. Just imagine… three clicks and you are where you want to be! There's so much good information here you will be back many times. So bookmark it immediately.

We'll show you how to save money on campgrounds, how to look at an RV, get better fuel mileage, deal with emergencies, measure your overswing, Canadian campground info, handle finances on the road, pack cooking liquids, drive over frost heaves, clean your fresh water tank, when to buy stuff at a rally, how to dump sewage, plus about a hundred other things. Whew!

The good news… we are not selling RV parts, no gadgets, no magic cleaners, no RVs (we do sell our books). We are just providing information that has been thoroughly researched, confirmed, and checked. This is information you can trust.

aboutrving.com